JUSTICE LEAGUE

VOL.2 OUTBREAK

"Some really thrilling artwork that establishes incredible scope and danger."
–IGN

DC UNIVERSE REBIRTH

JUSTICE LEAGUE

VOL. 1: The Extinction Machines

BRYAN HITCH
with TONY S. DANIEL

CYBORG VOL. 1:
THE IMITATION OF LIFE

GREEN LANTERNS VOL. 1:
RAGE PLANET

AQUAMAN VOL. 1:
THE DROWNING

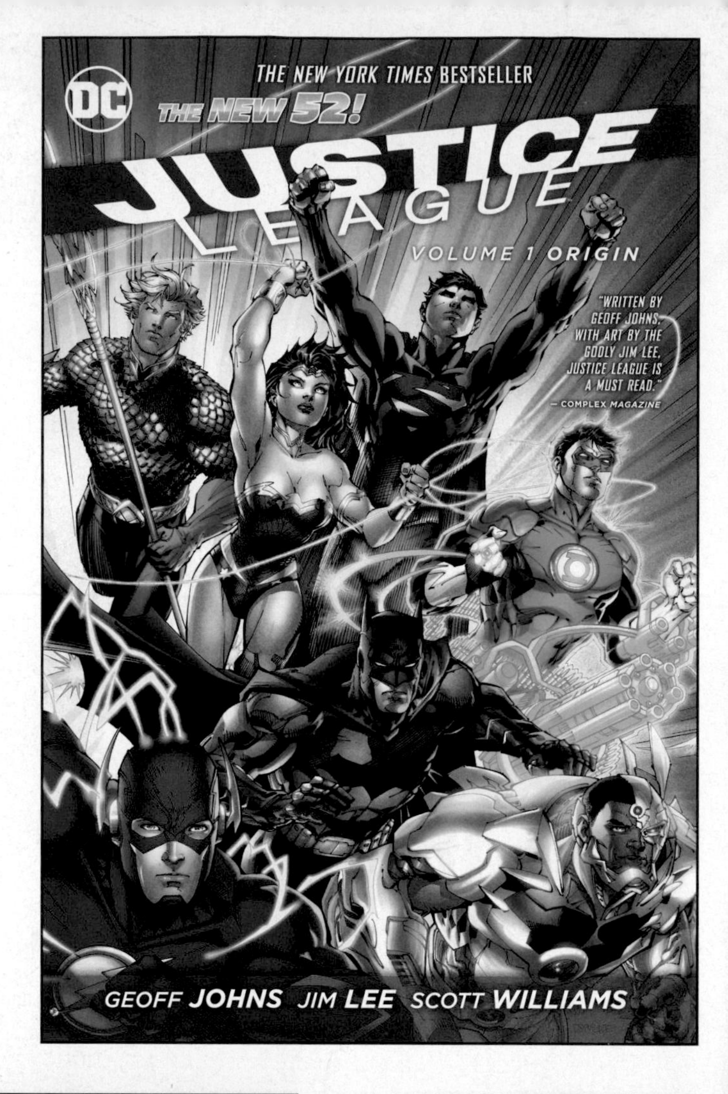

"Welcoming to new fans looking to get into superhero comics for the first time and old fans who gave up on the funny-books long ago."
– SCRIPPS HOWARD NEWS SERVICE

JUSTICE LEAGUE

VOL. 1: ORIGIN

GEOFF JOHNS
and JIM LEE

JUSTICE LEAGUE
VOL. 2: THE VILLAIN'S JOURNEY

JUSTICE LEAGUE
VOL. 3: THRONE OF ATLANTIS

READ THE ENTIRE EPIC!

JUSTICE LEAGUE VOL. 4: THE GRID

JUSTICE LEAGUE VOL. 5: FOREVER HEROES

JUSTICE LEAGUE VOL. 6: INJUSTICE LEAGUE

JUSTICE LEAGUE VOL. 7: DARKSEID WAR PART 1

JUSTICE LEAGUE VOL. 8: DARKSEID WAR PART 2

Get more DC graphic novels wherever comics and books are sold!

Layouts for JUSTICE LEAGUE #6 page 10

Layouts for JUSTICE LEAGUE #6 pages 8, 9, 15 and 20

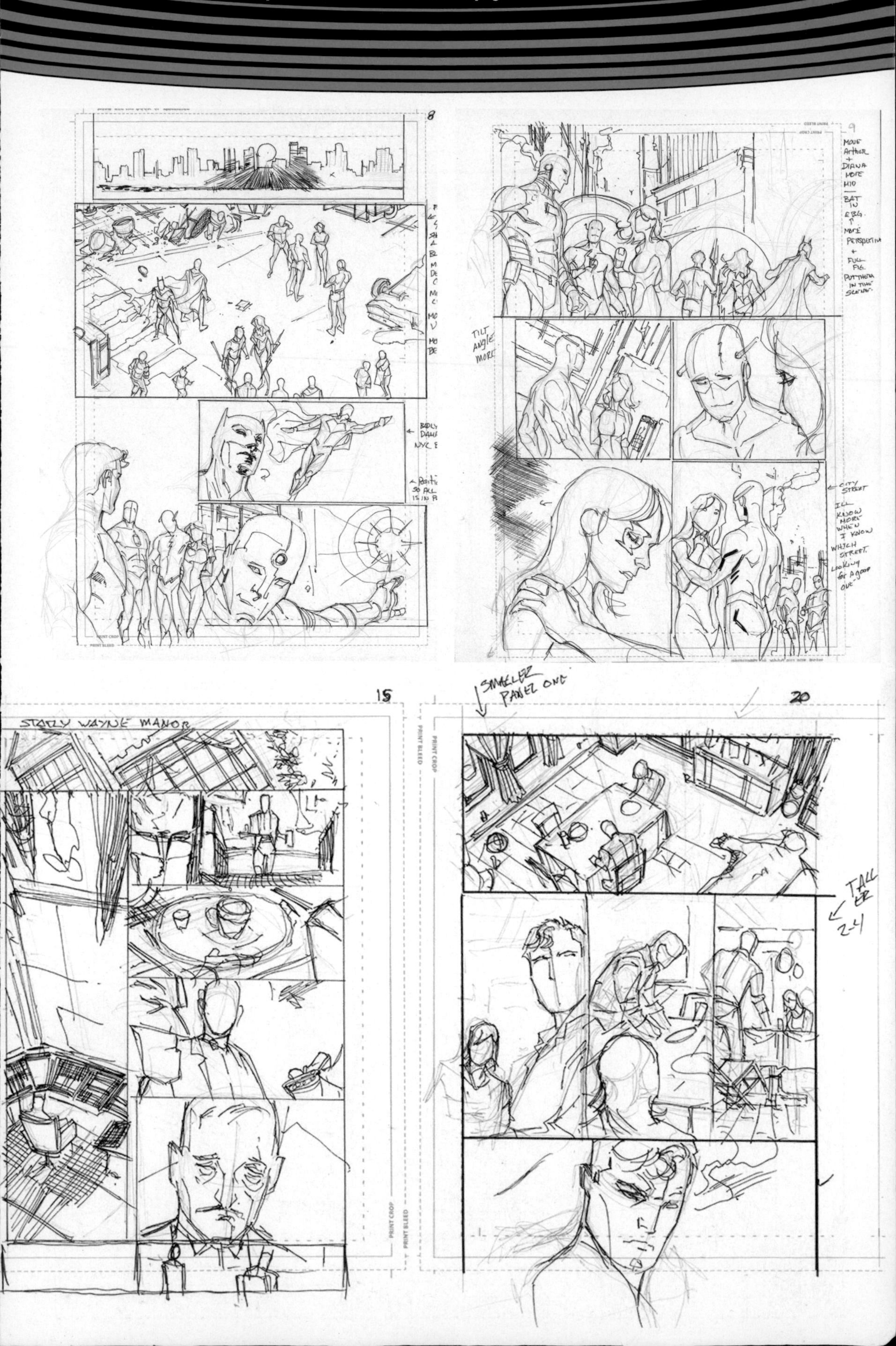

JUSTICE LEAGUE PAGE LAYOUTS BY MATTHEW CLARK

Layouts for JUSTICE LEAGUE #6 pages 4-7

JUSTICE LEAGUE #11
variant cover
by Yanick Paquette and
Nathan Fairbairn

JUSTICE LEAGUE #10 variant cover by Yanick Paquette and Nathan Fairbairn

JUSTICE LEAGUE #9 variant cover by Yanick Paquette and Nathan Fairbairn

JUSTICE LEAGUE #8 variant cover by Yanick Paquette and Nathan Fairbairn

JUSTICE LEAGUE #7 variant cover by Yanick Paquette and Nathan Fairbairn

JUSTICE LEAGUE #6 variant cover by Yanick Paquette and Nathan Fairbairn

JUSTICE LEAGUE

VARIANT COVER GALLERY

Paquette '16

AFTERMATH.
GREAT ENTRANCE. YOU BACK ON BOARD?
I CAME TO HELP, BARRY. I'LL ALWAYS DO THAT.
ALL THESE PEOPLE. THEIR WHOLE NEIGHBORHOOD IS GONE.
THEIR LIVES ARE RUINED.
WAYNE INDUSTRIES WILL TAKE CARE OF THEM. MAKE SURE THEY'RE LOOKED AFTER.
JAMES WILL HAVE A GOOD JOB. LILY'S EDUCATION WILL BE THE BEST I CAN GIVE HER.
ARE YOU GETTING SENTIMENTAL?
LOOK AT WHAT SHE DID. IMAGINE WHAT SHE'LL BE ABLE TO DO WITH THE PROPER GUIDANCE.
WITH WHAT WE ARE ABOUT TO FACE, WE CAN USE THAT.

YOU ONLY BOUGHT YOURSELF A FEW MINUTES, FLASH.
I'M GOING TO BURY THIS WHOLE PLACE AND ALL OF YOU WITH IT.
YOU CAN'T PUNCH THAT.

THERE'S NO WI-FI.
ALL THIS DESTRUCTION AND ENERGY WEAPONS. NO SIGNAL.
GOT TO FIND A WAY TO PUNCH THROUGH ALL THE INTERFERENCE.
USE ME.
BEST WI-FI IN THE WORLD.
NOW, LILY!
bHo7VDOS YCSdiepR 7oxqr85w aHYF16Jo Mos1207u Am4z015 L33t6JKq Hrt57MMk 4uk34jHH Jkla124r JLA1256jd $1b3rtwD 11tw3nty Tmm68jni xiz53jcp
WHAT DID YOU DO?
USED GENIE TO HACK THE PROGRAMMABLE CELLS THAT MAKE UP AMAZO'S BODY.
NOW AMAZO THINKS ALL OF YOU ARE THE JUSTICE LEAGUE.
HE'S ON OUR SIDE NOW.

REMEMBER, WE NEED THE GIRL AND THE IPAD. EVERYONE ELSE IS CANNON FODDER.
NO PRISONERS. NO MERCY.
THE LEAGUE CAN'T STAND AGAINST ALL OF US TOGETHER.
I'VE GOT AN IDEA!

NO!
EVERYONE, LISTEN!
WE HAVE THE MEANS TO BECOME RICHER THAN WE THOUGHT POSSIBLE.
THE MEANS TO TAKE ANYTHING WE WANT AND NEVER BE STOPPED, BUT WE HAVE TO WORK TOGETHER.
FOCUS ON GETTING PAST THE LEAGUE. WE NEED THE GIRL. JUST THE GIRL AND HER IPAD.

WE'D BETTER FALL BACK TO THE HOUSE.
THIS IS BAD ENOUGH WITHOUT THEM ALL WORKING TOGETHER.
NO MATTER WHAT HAPPENS, WE PROTECT THEM.
TO THE LAST.
TO THE *LAST.*

...TWO...

GNNNH
UNF... HEY!

...THREE...
THINK SHE BELONGS TO YOU.
YES.

EASY, JAMES. I NEED TO CHECK YOUR CONDITION. SCARECROW AND PSIMON WORKED YOU OVER PRETTY HARD.
...WHUH...
LILY! WHERE'S LILY...?
THEY TOOK HER, BUT IT'S OKAY. I PROMISE.
OKAY? HOW CAN IT BE OKAY?
MY FRIENDS ARE OUT THERE. THEY'RE THE BEST. THEY'LL GET HER.
THEY'LL LOOK AFTER HER.
LIKE THEY DID MY WIFE?
C'MON, BOBBY.
FLASH, YOU GOT MY DATA BURST. I GOT MAMMOTH COVERED...
NOW!
COUNT TO THREE...
ONE...

SEATTLE, WASHINGTON.
"...MISSING A PARTNER TO WATCH MY BACK..."
...DON'T KNOW WHERE THESE GUYS CAME FROM.
SAID THEY WERE PROMISED LEX LUTHOR'S FORTUNE TO KILL ME.
SEEMS TO BE THE DAY FOR IT.
WHAT DO YOU MEAN?
ON THE NEWS...
$%@!

I'VE GOT THESE TWO. YOU GO AND GET LILY BACK.
DESTROY THAT IPAD IF YOU HAVE TO. WE CAN'T LET THEM HAVE CONTROL OF GENIE. MAKE SURE IT CAN'T NETWORK OUT.
ALREADY ON IT.
CONTACTING THE OTHERS...

I'M IN PURSUIT OF GIZMO, PSIMON AND MAMMOTH. THEY HAVE LILY AND GENIE AND THEY KNOW ALL ABOUT WHAT IT CAN DO.
GONNA NEED ALL HANDS.
WE'RE PINNED DOWN HERE. WHERE'S SUPERMAN?
CALLED HIM, SAID HE WAS IN THE FORTRESS DEALING WITH A BREAKOUT OF THE PHANTOM ZONE.
GNH. GENIE?
MY GUESS.
GNAH!
DAMN IT! FEEL LIKE I'M MISSING A LIMB...

KEEP IT QUIET. WE CAN LEAVE ALL THE OTHERS TO KILL THE JUSTICE LEAGUE AND GET OUT WITH THIS GENIE THING.
IF I UNDERSTAND THE CODING CORRECTLY, IT CAN BYPASS ANY SECURITY AND GIVE US ANYTHING WE WANT.
IT COULD GIVE US THE WORLD.
WHICH DO YOU THINK WILL HURT THE MOST-- ME BURNING BATMAN OR YOU TURNING HIM INTO MERCURY?
I'M ALMOST AFRAID TO FIND OUT.
NO, BUT YOU WILL BE.
NO, NO, NO...
I CAN'T USE MY POWERS, SCARED THEY'LL BACKFIRE.
I HAVE TO GET AWAY--
OH GOD NO!
I'M BURNING, I'M BURNING!

WELL, IF I CAN'T GET *THROUGH* YOUR FORCE FIELD, I'LL JUST HAVE TO PUT YOU SOMEWHERE OUT OF TROUBLE.
TWO FOR THE PRICE OF ONE...
HEY, AQUAMAN...
...YOU *NAPPING* DOWN THERE?
I WAS JUST KEEPING HER OCCUPIED...
OH FOR...

ONE OF YOU IS GOING TO TELL US WHY THIS IS SO IMPORTANT THAT BATMAN AND THE OTHERS ARE RISKING THEIR LIVES FOR IT.
THEN YOU'RE GOING TO TELL ME WHAT WE CAN DO WITH IT.
OKAY. EVACUATION IS DONE. SURROUNDING NEIGHBORHOOD IS CLEAR TO A FIVE-MILE RADIUS.
IT'S CHAOS. BUT I CAN SEE PATTERNS IN IT.
THE LEAGUE IS BEING HIT HARD BUT I CAN SEE OUTCOMES, CALCULATE ODDS, RUN SCENARIOS.
HE'S THE WILD CARD. MAJOR DISASTER.
HE COULD BRING THE WHOLE NEIGHBORHOOD DOWN OR WORSE.
YOU MIGHT BE ABLE TO BREAK THROUGH MY SHIELDS, FLASH, BUT CAN YOU DO IT BEFORE I TURN THIS WHOLE NEIGHBORHOOD INTO A VOLCANIC CRATER?

UNF!
YOU HAVE TO GET THEM AND THAT GENIE THING IN THE IPAD OUT OF HERE.
THE STREET OUT THERE IS FULL OF SOME SERIOUSLY NASTY PEOPLE. WE CAN'T RISK THEM GETTING HOLD OF IT.
COVER US. WE'LL GO OUT THE BACK...
GNAH!
CAN'T RISK US GETTING HOLD OF WHAT?
GIZMO?
RUNNING SOME SORT OF COMPLEX ALGORITHMS.
AN A.I.?

EASY... HE'S DOWN.
I WAS TERRIFIED LILY AND BOBBY WERE GOING TO DIE. HE MADE ME SEE THAT.
I LOST THEIR MOM, I'M NOT GOING TO LOSE THEM.
IT'S OKAY, THEY'RE OKAY. JUST SCARED.
TAKE CARE OF THEM.
UNNH. OW...
SHH.
MAMMOTH.
...WHUH--?

HOW MANY TIMES, BATMAN? HOW MANY TIMES HAVE YOU BEEN CRIPPLED BY FEAR AT THE SCARECROW'S TOUCH?
DO YOU FEAR YOU'RE UNABLE TO PROTECT THESE PEOPLE?
FEAR YOU'LL WATCH THEM DIE, UNABLE TO LIFT A FINGER TO HELP?
THEY WILL. THEY'LL DIE, TERRIFIED TO THE END.
IT'S SO DELICIOUS, YOUR HELPLESSNESS--
GAH!
DAMN FREAK!
I'LL KILL FOR WHAT YOU--

GURK... CAN'T... RUN...
GNNN...
THE REST OF YOU FINISH HIM WHILE I HOLD HIS MIND!
OH YEAH!
PSIMON. PSYCHIC, TELEKINETIC, MIND BLASTS. NOT TO BE TAKEN LIGHTLY.
GAH!
YAAAAAH!
GNNH!
WORKING ON IT.
THIS IS GETTING OUT OF CONTROL. IT'S GOING TO DESTROY THE NEIGHBORHOOD.
MAPS SAY A SCHOOL IS THREE MILES FROM HERE. EVAC THE HOUSES IN THAT AREA, GIVE US A CLEAR ZONE. I'LL HANDLE THESE GUYS.
OKAY. BE BACK IN A MINUTE OR TWO.
DON'T GET KILLED.

GIGANTA.
COLDSNAP AND HEATSTROKE.
GIRDER.
A FEW OTHERS WE ALREADY TOOK CARE OF.
OH, AND AMAZO.
HE CAN MIMIC ANY SUPERPOWER HE ENCOUNTERS, INCLUDING THOSE OF THE JUSTICE LEAGUE. WE'RE DOWN A GREEN LANTERN AND SUPERMAN HASN'T RESPONDED.
WE ARE IN DEEP @$%&.

THE FEARSOME FIVE: PSIMON, MAMMOTH, JINX, GIZMO AND SHIMMER.
PLASTIQUE.
MAJOR DISASTER.

OUTBREAK
CONCLUSION

BRYAN HITCH WRITER / NEIL EDWARDS PENCILLER / DANIEL HENRIQUES INKER
ADRIANO LUCAS COLORIST / RICHARD STARKINGS & COMICRAFT LETTERING
FERNANDO PASARIN, MATT RYAN & BRAD ANDERSON COVER
YANICK PAQUETTE & NATHAN FAIRBAIRN VARIANT COVER
AMEDEO TURTURRO & DIEGO LOPEZ ASSISTANT EDITORS / BRIAN CUNNINGHAM EDITOR

WE NEED TO END THIS QUICKLY. THESE HOUSES ARE FILLED WITH PEOPLE, FAMILIES.
AGREED.
THEY ARE POWERFUL, BUT IF NO OTHERS ARE INVOLVED WE SHOULD BE...
AMAZO. ABILITY TO DUPLICATE METAHUMAN POWERS.
OKAY. NOW WE'RE IN TROUBLE.

YES.
WE HAVE THIS.

...NO...
...SCARECROW...
ARE YOU AFRAID YET? YOU SHOULD BE!
I'LL DANCE ON YOUR TWITCHING CORPSES WHEN YOU'VE SCARED YOURSELVES TO DEATH!

BACK INSIDE, QUICKLY.
I'LL KEEP THE FAMILY SAFE. THE REST OF YOU...
LILY, YOU NEED TO SHUT GENIE DOWN SO NO MORE SHOW UP.
WE CAN AT LEAST MAKE SURE THIS DOESN'T GET ANY WORSE.
OKAY, LET ME--

AAAAAAHHHH!
NO! PLEASE GOD, NO!

WHAT IS IT...?
NO, KEEP AWAY!
NO, NO, NO...

PLASTIQUE. EXPLOSIVE POWERS.
GIRDER. INVULNERABILITY AND SUPER-STRENGTH.
PSIMON. TELEKINESIS. TELEPATHY.
COLDSNAP. COLD POWERS.
SHIMMER. ABILITY TO TRANSMUTE MATTER.
MAJOR DISASTER. CAUSES EARTHQUAKES.

GIGANTA. SIZE ALTERATION, SUPERHUMAN STRENGTH AND DURABILITY.
GIZMO. GENIUS-LEVEL INTELLECT.
HEATSTROKE. HEAT AND FLAME.
JINX. ELEMENTAL SORCERESS.
MAMMOTH. SUPER-STRENGTH. RESISTANCE TO PHYSICAL HARM.

REALLY?
YOU GUYS FINISHED GOING ALL STAR TREK OVER THERE?
SIMON, YOU AND ME NEED TO GO NOW. DRAW ANYBODY WHO'S COMING AWAY.
IT'S US THEY'RE TRACKING.
MULTIPLE ASSAILANTS.
TACTICAL INFORMATION COMING IN...

BATMAN'S RIGHT. THEY'RE COMING HERE FOR US. WE NEED TO GET AWAY FROM POPULATED AREAS SO WE CAN DEAL WITH THIS PROPERLY.
WE DON'T KNOW HOW MANY COULD BE COMING. THESE AREN'T THE TYPE OF PEOPLE THAT WORRY ABOUT COLLATERAL DAMAGE.
WE'LL COME BACK, LILY. WHEN WE'VE FINISHED, WE'LL COME BACK, I PROMISE.
OKAY?
OKAY.
UNNNH...
WHY ARE YOU ALL FALLING? WHAT'S GOING ON?
UGNH...
THE JUSTICE LEAGUE!
HOW CAN YOU FIGHT WHEN YOU DON'T KNOW WHICH WAY IS UP?
COUNT VERTIGO. HYPNOSIS. CAN CONFUSE AND WARP PEOPLE'S SENSES.

BOXING GLOVE. CLASSIC.
GIANT WOMAN? LARGE LASS?
WAIT, I GOT IT. MOUNTAINOUS MARY?
GIGANTA.
HUH.
OH CRAP.
THAT'S MRS. CASTERMAN'S HOUSE. SHE WENT TO HER DAUGHTER'S THIS WEEKEND.
WE CAN'T DO THIS HERE.

SEVEN HUNDRED FIFTY BILLION IS ON THE TABLE AND ALL I GOT TO DO IS KILL THE JUSTICE LEAGUE.
I'LL TAKE THOSE ODDS!
SIX TO ONE? CHANCE IN A MILLION.
REALLY? DOUBLE DOWN? THAT'S IT?
HADDA ASK.

THAT'S OKAY, WE'VE BEATEN THEM ALL BEFORE.
NOT ALL AT THE SAME TIME.
IT'S JUST A GAME, THOUGH, RIGHT?

TO HIM? YES. BUT THIS GENIE OPERATES IN THE REAL WORLD, DOESN'T IT?
WELL, YEAH.
RIGHT, WE'D BETTER GO AND STOP ALL THIS BEFORE IT BECOMES SOMETHING PEOPLE COULD BE HURT BY.

WE NEED TO SHUT THIS GENIE DOWN.
HANG ON, THERE'S SOMETHING ELSE.
GENIE HAS TOLD ALL THESE VILLAINS WHERE TO FIND US.

WHAT DO YOU MEAN?
IT LEFT BEHIND A TRACE SIGNAL IN THE THINGS IT JUST HACKED.
YOU AND ME, VIC, RIGHT?
THAT MEANS IT KNOWS WE'RE HERE. RIGHT HERE--

SO YOU TOLD GENIE ALL ABOUT YOUR GAMES?
YEAH. IT SAID IT COULD HELP ME WITH THE GAME.
IT'S STILL ACTIVE.

WHAT'S IT DOING?
DON'T WANT TO CONNECT DIRECTLY, SO GIVE ME A...
OKAY. IT'S SETTING UP A NEW GAME. LOOKS LIKE IT'S CALLED "VILLAINS."

YEAH, WE WERE GOING TO PLAY IT NEXT.
WHAT'S THE GAME, BOBBY? WHAT HAPPENS?
ALL THE VILLAINS JOIN TOGETHER AND BEAT UP THE JUSTICE LEAGUE.

RIGHT. WELL, MAYBE WE SHOULDN'T PLAY THAT GAME RIGHT NOW, OKAY?
MIGHT BE TOO LATE FOR THAT.

WHAT DO YOU MEAN?
THIS "GAME" HAS BEEN RUNNING FOR A WHILE. WANT TO KNOW WHAT HAPPENS?
SOME OF THE WORST VILLAINS WE'VE ALL FACED ARE LOCATED AND OFFERED LEX LUTHOR'S AND BRUCE WAYNE'S FORTUNES TO FIND US AND KILL US.
DOZENS OF THEM.

YOU TOOK MY IPAD AGAIN, BOBBY?
WHAT'VE YOU BEEN DOING?
I WAS JUST PLAYING. YOU SAID I COULD.
IT'S OKAY, BOBBY. LET ME JUST TAKE A LOOK.

IT'S ON YOUR GENIE APP, LIL.
IT WAS TALKING TO ME, ASKING ME QUESTIONS.
I THOUGHT IT WAS NICE.

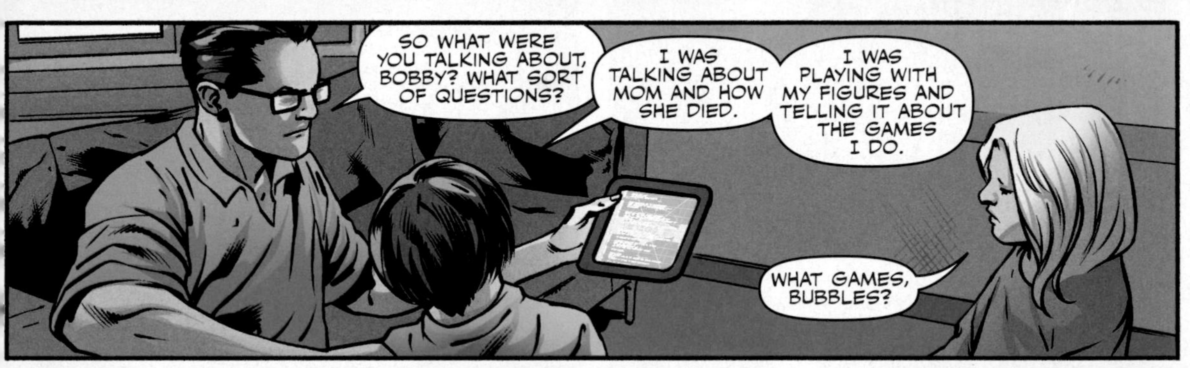
SO WHAT WERE YOU TALKING ABOUT, BOBBY? WHAT SORT OF QUESTIONS?
I WAS TALKING ABOUT MOM AND HOW SHE DIED.
I WAS PLAYING WITH MY FIGURES AND TELLING IT ABOUT THE GAMES I DO.
WHAT GAMES, BUBBLES?

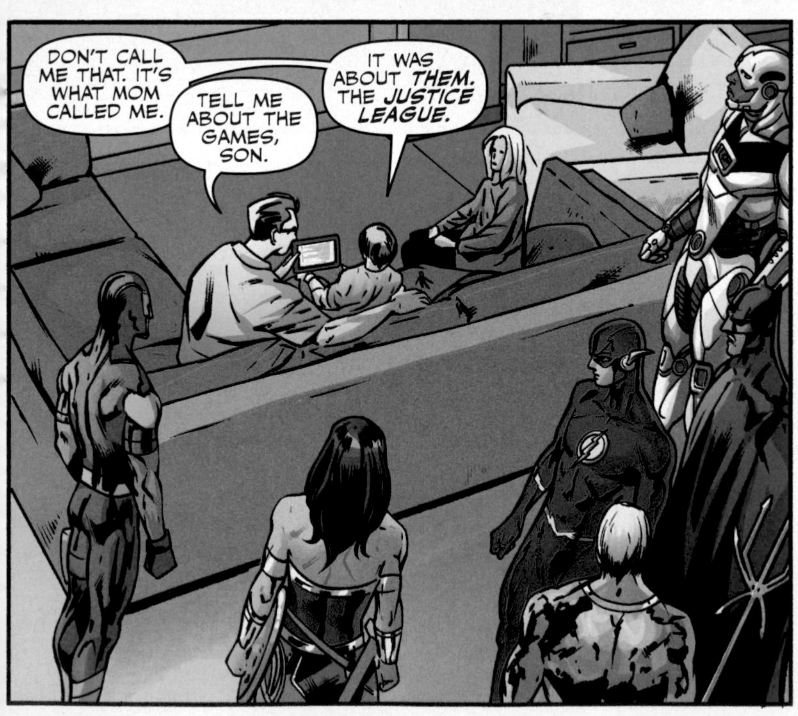
DON'T CALL ME THAT. IT'S WHAT MOM CALLED ME.
TELL ME ABOUT THE GAMES, SON.
IT WAS ABOUT THEM. THE JUSTICE LEAGUE.

IT WAS ABOUT WHAT WOULD HAPPEN IF THEY LOST AND MOM DIDN'T DIE. IT WAS JUST A GAME.
I KNOW, BOBBY, I KNOW.

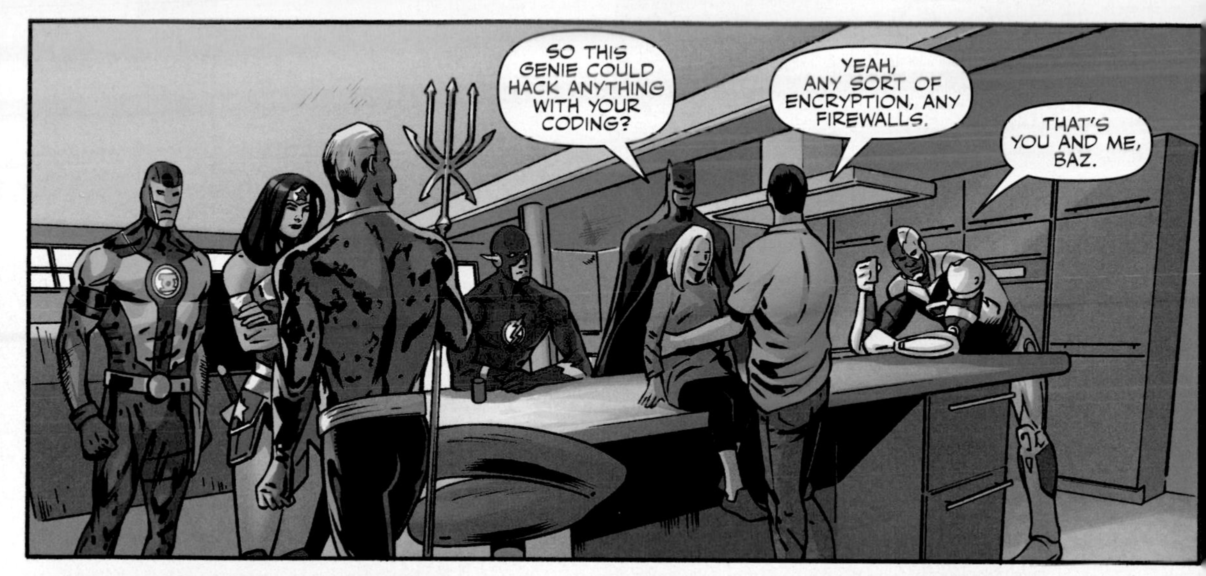
SO THIS GENIE COULD HACK ANYTHING WITH YOUR CODING?
YEAH, ANY SORT OF ENCRYPTION, ANY FIREWALLS.
THAT'S YOU AND ME, BAZ.

SO WE NEARLY GOT OUR BUTTS HANDED TO US BY GOOGLE?
WHY WOULD YOU USE THIS GENIE TO HARM US?
WHO, ME? NO! I DIDN'T DO ANYTHING!
I JUST PUT THE APP ON MY IPAD YESTERDAY. I WAS GOING TO TRY IT OUT ON SOME SCHOOL FRIENDS.

CAN I SEE IT?
YEAH, IT WAS JUST ON HERE...
...OH.

WHAT?

LILY?
WHAT, WHY?
I WAS JUST LOOKING THROUGH MOM'S STUFF AFTER... Y'KNOW. I FOUND YOUR NOTEBOOKS.
YOU COULD UNDERSTAND THAT STUFF?
DAD, I'VE WATCHED EVERY LINE OF CODE YOU PROGRAMMED SINCE I WAS BORN. I LEARNED TO READ THAT BEFORE I READ DR. SEUSS.
I KNOW, I MEAN I KNOW YOU LIKED PROGRAMMING. ALWAYS FIDDLING.
THAT DATING APP WAS HUGE IN SCHOOL, RIGHT?
YEAH, 'CEPT ALISON GRAHAM ENDED UP SELECTING DAVID BATES, THE UGLIEST, SHORTEST KID IN SCHOOL, AS HER DREAM DATE.
RIGHT. YEAH.
WHY WOULD YOU BE USING MY CODING?
IT'S A BOT. A NEXT-GEN A.I. A SEARCH ENGINE THAT COULD FIND WHAT YOU WANT BEFORE YOU KNEW YOU WANTED IT.
BUT MY ANTI-ENCRYPTION STUFF?
COULD GET ANYWHERE SEARCH ENGINES CAN'T. THIS WAS DIFFERENT THOUGH.
IMAGINE SOMETHING YOU CAN TALK TO LIKE A FRIEND THAT CAN WORK OUT WHAT YOU WANT AND PROVIDE A WAY OF DOING IT. LIKE THE IMPOSSIBLE-TO-FIND TICKETS OR DINNER RESERVATIONS.
HOW LONG DO WE SPEND LOOKING THROUGH SEARCH RESULTS? IMAGINE A SEARCH ENGINE THAT COULD ASK US A FEW QUESTIONS, INTUITIVELY FIGURE OUT EXACTLY WHAT WE WANT AND JUST GIVE US THE RIGHT RESULT EVERY TIME.
I CALLED IT *GENIE.* IT WAS SUPPOSED TO GRANT WISHES.
THOUGHT IT MIGHT BE SOMETHING WE COULD MAKE A BIT OF MONEY OFF OF IF I SOLD IT TO DEVELOPERS.

COULD ANYBODY YOU KNOW HAVE USED THE CODE?
I WAS ALWAYS CAREFUL WITH IT. IT COULD LITERALLY HACK ANY SORT OF ENCRYPTION SOFTWARE, SO I KEPT IT SAFE.
I WASN'T GOING TO LET IT FALL INTO THE WRONG HANDS, LIKE THE GOVERNMENT OR THE MILITARY. CIA.

WHERE WAS IT KEPT? COULD *YOU* HAVE BEEN HACKED? HAD THE CODE STOLEN?
I KEPT IT SAFE FROM HACKERS. IT'S WRITTEN DOWN IN A NOTEBOOK I KEEP IN A BOX IN MY BEDROOM. CAN'T HACK PEN AND PAPER.
IT'S STILL THERE. I GOT IT OUT TO START THE HACK THIS WEEK.

DAD?
NOT NOW, LILY. CAN YOU SEE TO YOUR BROTHER?

WELL, SOMEBODY USED IT AND WROTE IT INTO THE A.I. THAT GOT THROUGH OUR SECURITY AND TRIED TO KILL US. TRIED TO CRASH OUR SATELLITE INTO SAN FRANCISCO.
THAT WASN'T ME.
DAD!

HANG ON, LILY.
MAYBE I CAN HELP YOU FIND WHOEVER DID THIS. IF THEY'RE USING MY CODE, I'D LIKE TO KNOW HOW THEY GOT IT.
DAD!

WHAT'S THE MATTER LILY? I'M TALKING!
IT WAS ME.
I TOOK YOUR CODE.

IS THAT WHY YOU ATTACKED US? REVENGE?
WHAT? NO. I DIDN'T ATTACK ANYBODY. NOT YET. AND EVEN THEN, IT WAS GOING TO BE LEXCORP, MAYBE A FEW OTHERS. WAYNE, GUYS LIKE THAT.
YOU WERE GOING TO ATTACK LEX LUTHOR?

NO, NOT HIM PERSONALLY, JUST TAKE SOME OF HIS MONEY AND GIVE IT TO THE VICTIMS OF THE KINDRED. PEOPLE WHO NEEDED IT. PEOPLE WHO HAVE BEEN STRUGGLING SINCE THE KINDRED. PEOPLE LIKE US.
I HAVEN'T EVEN DONE IT YET. HONESTLY. I HAVEN'T HURT ANYBODY.
HE'S TELLING THE TRUTH.

WE WERE ATTACKED BY A SELF-GENERATING A.I. IT WAS TRYING TO KILL US.
ITS ROOT CODE WAS YOURS. JESSE JAMES', FROM YOUR HACKING DAYS.
YOU KNOW ABOUT ALL THAT? I WAS JUST GOING TO TAKE SOME MONEY. WHY WOULD I TRY TO KILL YOU?

YOUR WIFE?
IT'S TRULY THE WORST THING THAT COULD HAVE HAPPENED TO US AS A FAMILY, BUT THAT DOESN'T MAKE ME A KILLER. I'D NEVER HURT ANYBODY.

DON'T BLAME US?
FOR DIANE. FOR MY WIFE.
PUT SOME COFFEE ON, LILY. THERE'RE SOME ENERGY DRINKS IN THE CUPBOARD.

SHE WAS ONE OF THE PEOPLE WHO GOT CAUGHT UP IN THAT KINDRED STUFF A FEW WEEKS AGO.
STARTED TALKING FUNNY, ABOUT STOLEN SPEED, AND WALKED OUT THE DOOR. SHE DIDN'T LOOK BACK.
THAT'S THE LAST TIME WE SAW HER...
ALIVE, ANYWAY.
I'M VERY SORRY FOR YOUR LOSS.

REALLY?
DON'T YOU GET NUMB TO ALL THAT BIG STUFF? ALIENS, MONSTERS, MASS DESTRUCTION? WHAT ARE WE TO PEOPLE LIKE YOU?
EVERYTHING, MAN.
THE REASON WE DO ALL OF IT.

I WAS JUST TRYING TO HELP EVERYBODY. WE AREN'T THE ONLY ONES AFFECTED.
THE FRASERS UP THE STREET HAVEN'T BEEN ABLE TO WORK.
THEY WERE ALREADY IN DEBT AND THEIR MORTGAGE COMPANY WANTS TO FORECLOSE.

MIKE AND LINDA FRIEDMAN AT SCHOOL SAID THEIR DAD KEEPS BLACKING OUT AND STUFF.
IT'S NOT JUST US WHO WERE AFFECTED BY ALL THAT KINDRED STUFF. WE WERE JUST THE ONLY ONES TO LOSE SOMEBODY.

WHY ARE YOU HERE? WHY'VE I GOT THE JUSTICE LEAGUE IN MY HOUSE?
OH MY GOD, I *HAVE* THE JUSTICE LEAGUE IN MY HOUSE.
WHAT COULD ALL OF YOU POSSIBLY WANT WITH ME?
TWO ACTS OF CYBER-TERRORISM, SPECIFICALLY TARGETED AGAINST US. ONE OF WHICH COULD HAVE LED TO CITYWIDE DESTRUCTION.
DAD?
IT WASN'T ME.
DAD, IN THE GARAGE...?
LILY, NO, IT WASN'T ME.
IS THAT WHAT YOU THINK OF ME? THAT I'D DO SOMETHING LIKE THAT?
CYBER-TERRORISM? HURT PEOPLE?
DAD, YOU'VE BEEN IN THERE FOR DAYS. YOU SAID YOU HAD TO TAKE CARE OF SOMETHING.
WHAT'S GOING ON?
YES, EXPLAIN.
LOOK, I WASN'T, I MEAN, NOT THIS.
I WAS JUST TRYING TO SORT US OUT, THAT'S ALL. I LOST MY JOB LAST MONTH BEFORE... BEFORE...
I'M SORRY.
JAMES, IT'S OKAY.
START FROM THE BEGINNING.
OKAY. RIGHT.
I DON'T BLAME ANY OF YOU FOR WHAT HAPPENED, YOU KNOW?

DO WE HAVE TO DO THIS OUT HERE? BAD ENOUGH IN FRONT OF MY KIDS...
...CAN YOU COME INSIDE?
...TOLD YOU HE WAS UP TO SOMETHING...
AFTER WHAT HAPPENED TO HIS WIFE, DIANE. SUCH A SHAME...
I DON'T SUPPOSE ANYBODY WANTS COFFEE.
SOMETHING STRONGER?
I COULD TAKE AN ENERGY DRINK OR TWO IF YOU...
WHAT?

OUTBREAK PART THREE

BRYAN HITCH WRITER / NEIL EDWARDS PENCILLER / DANIEL HENRIQUES INKER
ADRIANO LUCAS COLORIST / RICHARD STARKINGS & COMICRAFT LETTERING
SCOT EATON, WAYNE FAUCHER & BRAD ANDERSON COVER / YANICK PAQUETTE & NATHAN FAIRBAIRN VARIANT COVER
AMEDEO TURTURRO & DIEGO LOPEZ ASSISTANT EDITORS / BRIAN CUNNINGHAM EDITOR

EATON
FAUCHER
BA

OUTBREAK PART TWO

BRYAN HITCH WRITER / NEIL EDWARDS PENCILLER / DANIEL HENRIQUES INKER
TONY AVIÑA COLORIST / RICHARD STARKINGS & COMICRAFT LETTERING
FERNANDO PASARIN, MATT RYAN & BRAD ANDERSON COVER
YANICK PAQUETTE & NATHAN FAIRBAIRN VARIANT COVER
AMEDEO TURTURRO & DIEGO LOPEZ ASSISTANT EDITORS / BRIAN CUNNINGHAM EDITOR

ANYBODY WANT TO TELL ME WHAT JUST HAPPENED?
WE WERE HACKED. DON'T KNOW BY WHAT YET. THE VIRUS GOT INTO YOUR RING AND IT TRIED TO KILL ALL OF US.
DIDN'T TRY TO KILL ME. I GOT A BOXING GLOVE.
THAT'S WHAT I REALIZED WHEN DIANA WAS TALKING ABOUT KILLING YOU.
YOUR RING'S MOST BASIC PROGRAMMING IS TO PROTECT ITS WEARER, RIGHT?
WE WENT AT YOU WITH WHAT APPEARED TO BE DEADLY FORCE HOPING YOUR RING WOULD REVERT TO FACTORY SETTINGS AND LOSE THE VIRUS.
FACTORY SETTINGS?
IT'S NOT A DAMN IPHONE.
WAIT, WHAT IF IT HADN'T WORKED?
LET'S JUST FOCUS ON THE POSITIVE, RIGHT?
YOU THOUGHT ABOUT KILLING ME?
GUYS, I GOT BATMAN...

HOLY CRA--
UNF...
BE READY, THE RING COULD ATTACK AGAIN...

EMERGENCY PROTOCOLS INITIATED.
...WHOA...!

REBOOTING.
SYSTEMS ONLINE...
OW. WAIT... YEAH, OW.
REALLY BIG OW.
I'M BACK ONLINE. ANYBODY THERE? WE NEED TO FIGURE OUT HOW TO STOP SIMON'S POWER RING...
I'M ON THE GROUND NEARBY BUT I GOT NOTHING. I'M WORRIED ABOUT HURTING HIM.
VIC? YOU OKAY? I LEFT YOU A MESSAGE...
REALLY? HANG ON...
VIC? BARRY. GOT AN IDEA. LISTEN...
...YOU SERIOUS?
DEADLY.
...UNF...
...WHAT'S...WHAT'S HAPPENING...?

DOES ANYBODY HAVE ANY IDEA HOW WE CAN PUT A STOP TO THIS?
I'D HATE TO KILL SIMON.
THAT'S A JOKE, RIGHT? OF COURSE YOU'RE JOKING.
WAIT, HANG ON! DIANA, THAT'S GENIUS!
WE'RE GOING TO KILL SIMON? I WASN'T SERIOUS, FLASH...
JUST LISTEN, LOOPING ARTHUR IN, TOO. CAN'T RAISE VIC...
MAKE IT QUICK...

REBOOT: UNAVAILABLE.
SHUT DOWN: UNAVAILABLE.
...WRONG...
MOTOR FUNCTIONS: INTERMITTENT.
GAAAAAH!

YEAH. WE'RE ALL "FINE."
YOU. ME. BOBBY.
DON'T.

MOM.
LILY, DON'T. PLEASE.

BOBBY NEEDS YOU, DAD. WE BOTH DO. WE JUST GOT BACK FROM MOM'S FUNERAL.
WHY ARE YOU EVEN IN HERE?
WHY AREN'T YOU WITH US?
I JUST HAVE TO TAKE CARE OF SOMETHING.

TAKE CARE OF US.
PLEASE?

I WILL, LILY. I PROMISE I WILL.
JUST NEED TO FINISH THIS FIRST.
JUST ONE THING.

DENVER. THE PALMER HOUSE.
"...BUT WE CAN'T LET THIS GO. HE GOT TOO CLOSE TO US. WE NEED TO SHUT IT DOWN."
LILY, WHERE'S YOUR IPAD? I WAS PLAYING ON IT...
I NEED IT. I GOTTA SEE DAD. WATCH POKÉMON OR SOMETHING.
LILY... I WANT TO PLAY...
LATER, BOBBY, OKAY?
DAD?
DADDY?
I TOLD YOU NOT TO COME IN HERE. I'M BUSY WITH THINGS.
WHAT THINGS?
JUST THINGS. THINGS THAT WILL HELP US.
I THOUGHT YOU MAYBE WANTED COFFEE OR BREAKFAST OR SOMETHING.
I'M OKAY. I'M FINE.

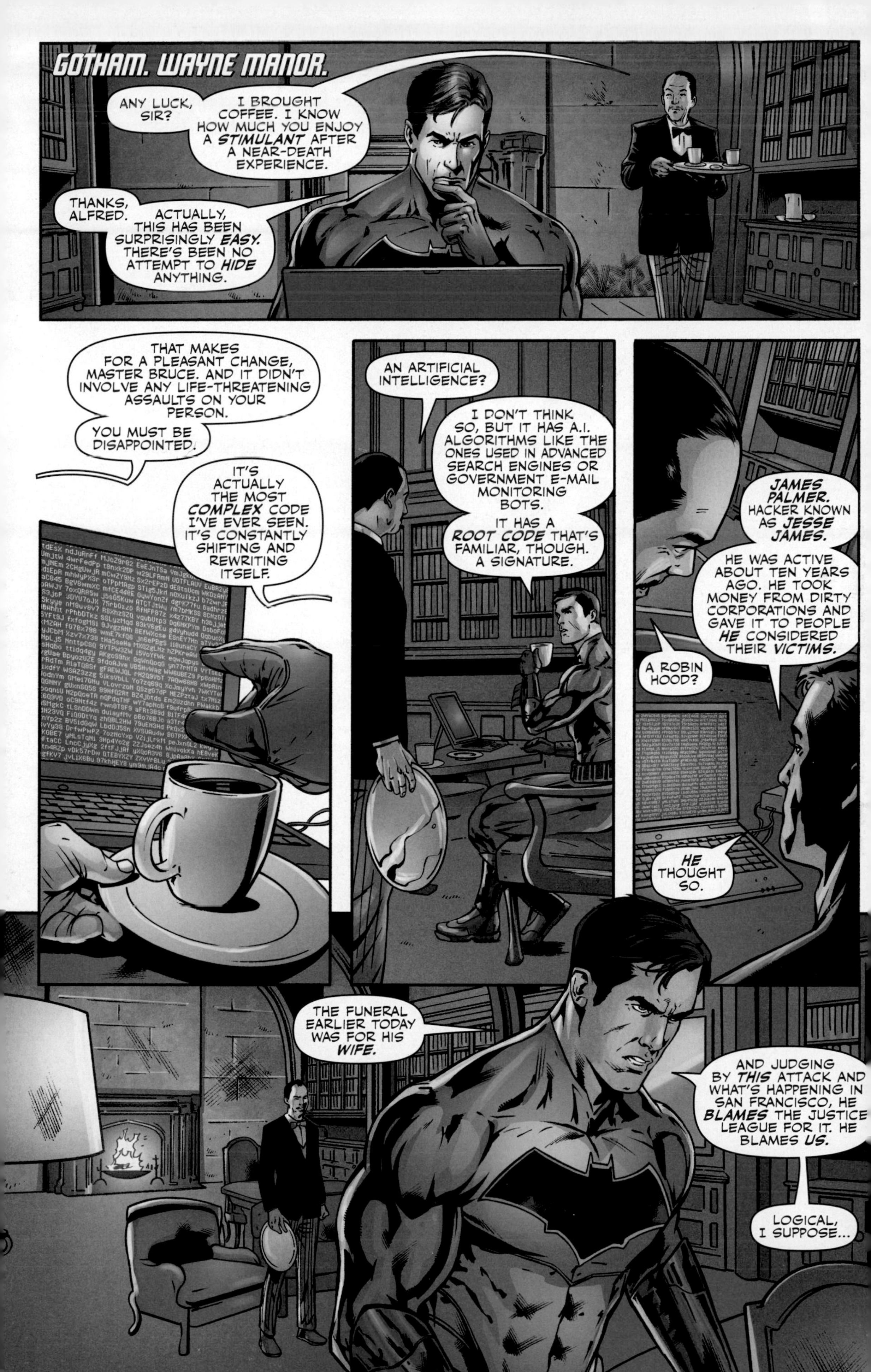
GOTHAM. WAYNE MANOR.
ANY LUCK, SIR?
I BROUGHT COFFEE. I KNOW HOW MUCH YOU ENJOY A STIMULANT AFTER A NEAR-DEATH EXPERIENCE.
THANKS, ALFRED.
ACTUALLY, THIS HAS BEEN SURPRISINGLY EASY. THERE'S BEEN NO ATTEMPT TO HIDE ANYTHING.
THAT MAKES FOR A PLEASANT CHANGE, MASTER BRUCE. AND IT DIDN'T INVOLVE ANY LIFE-THREATENING ASSAULTS ON YOUR PERSON.
YOU MUST BE DISAPPOINTED.
IT'S ACTUALLY THE MOST COMPLEX CODE I'VE EVER SEEN. IT'S CONSTANTLY SHIFTING AND REWRITING ITSELF.
AN ARTIFICIAL INTELLIGENCE?
I DON'T THINK SO, BUT IT HAS A.I. ALGORITHMS LIKE THE ONES USED IN ADVANCED SEARCH ENGINES OR GOVERNMENT E-MAIL MONITORING BOTS.
IT HAS A ROOT CODE THAT'S FAMILIAR, THOUGH. A SIGNATURE.
JAMES PALMER. HACKER KNOWN AS JESSE JAMES.
HE WAS ACTIVE ABOUT TEN YEARS AGO. HE TOOK MONEY FROM DIRTY CORPORATIONS AND GAVE IT TO PEOPLE HE CONSIDERED THEIR VICTIMS.
A ROBIN HOOD?
HE THOUGHT SO.
THE FUNERAL EARLIER TODAY WAS FOR HIS WIFE.
AND JUDGING BY THIS ATTACK AND WHAT'S HAPPENING IN SAN FRANCISCO, HE BLAMES THE JUSTICE LEAGUE FOR IT. HE BLAMES US.
LOGICAL, I SUPPOSE...

JUST IN CASE YOU DON'T KNOW WHAT THAT MEANS...

THIS OCEAN IS MINE. HERE, I AM KING.
I RULE.

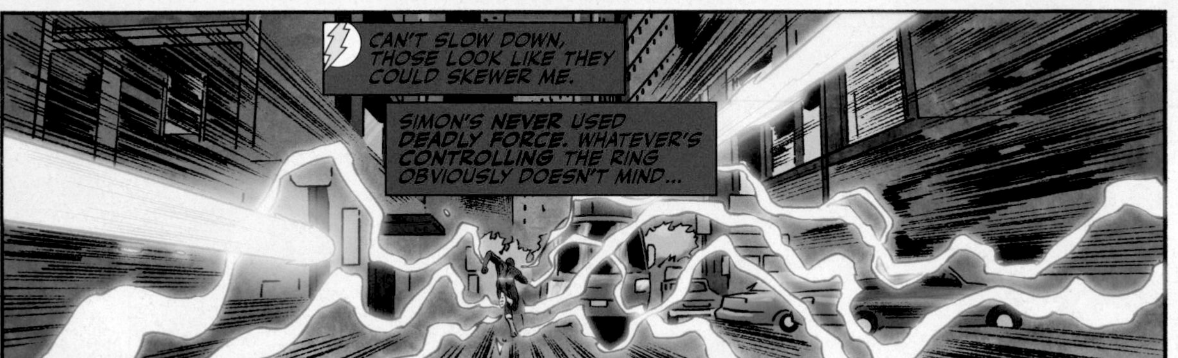
CAN'T SLOW DOWN, THOSE LOOK LIKE THEY COULD SKEWER ME.
SIMON'S NEVER USED DEADLY FORCE. WHATEVER'S CONTROLLING THE RING OBVIOUSLY DOESN'T MIND...

GOTTA BE SOME WAY OF SHUTTING THIS ALL DOWN.

C'MON, BARRY. FIGURE IT OUT...

CAN'T RUN FOREVER...

REBOOT. UNAVAILABLE.
SHUT DOWN. UNAVAILABLE.
...SCREW THIS...
MOTOR FUNCTIONS: INTERMITTENT.
CYBORG, HUH...?
...NOT TODAY...
...I'M A MAN... FIRST...
...AND I'M NOT GOING TO BE CONTROLLED BY THE REST OF ME...
I'VE FOUGHT THE REAL CREATURES FROM THE DARKEST OF ALL MYTHS.
YOU ARE JUST PUPPETS OF LIGHT!
WE NEED TO FIND A WAY OF SHUTTING THAT RING DOWN!

RUN?
OH, I'LL RUN. BUT THAT'S LIGHT CHASING ME...
IT'S GOING TO CATCH ME EVENTUALLY. THAT'S JUST PHYSICS.
DRY LAND, IN THE AIR, THESE CONSTRUCTS HAVE THE ADVANTAGE...
...LET'S SEE WHAT I CAN DO DOWN HERE...

UNF.
...OH FOR ZEUS' SAKE...
GIANT HANDS, GIANT BOXING GLOVES. DOES EVERY GREEN LANTERN DO THIS...?
AND SEA-FOOD? I HATE SEAFOOD.
ESPECIALLY WHEN IT'S GREEN...
FLASH?
RUN.

UNH.
MORE LIKE IT...
HEY, NOT TOO SHABBY, SIMON.
...ABOUT TIME...
...HNF...
THEY'RE FADING.
THAT'S BETTER.
RIGHT, VIC, LET'S SEE IF WE CAN HELP SORT YOU...

SORRY!
DON'T KNOW WHAT'S... GOING ON.
IT WON'T DO WHAT I'M TELLING IT TO DO...
...NEVER WOULD HAVE HAPPENED TO JORDAN...
REBOOT. UNAVAILABLE.
SHUT DOWN. UNAVAILABLE.
AVAILABLE MOTOR FUNCTIONS: INTERMITTENT.
THE VIRUS... GOT INTO YOUR RING THROUGH ME...
...GOT IT THROUGH NEWS FEED... IT'S SHUTTING ME DOWN...
THIS IS MY RING, DAMMIT.
MINE.

...RUN, GET AWAY...!
GAH!
BAZ! GET YOUR RING UNDER CONTROL!

SAN FRANCISCO, CALIFORNIA.
...OUTTA THE WAY...
...THE HELL...?

DOES ANYTHING NEED TO BE STITCHED OR ANY BONES RESET, SIR? I COULD DO THAT BEFORE MAKING SOME TEA.
I'M FINE, ALFRED. I'VE HAD WORSE DAYS.
INDEED, SIR, AND NIGHTS, TOO.

I'LL TAKE THE WIRELESS CARD OUT OF THIS LAPTOP SO WHATEVER'S IN THIS CODE WILL STAY ON A CLOSED SYSTEM.
THEN I CAN RUN SOME DIAGNOSTICS ON IT AND TRY TO TRACE ITS ORIGINS.

TURN THE TV ON, ALFRED. THE NEWS. LET'S SEE IF WE WERE THE ONLY TARGETS OR IF THERE WERE ANY WIDER EFFECTS.

A LARGE-SCALE CYBERATTACK? BANKS? GOVERNMENTS? THAT SORT OF THING?
MAYBE I SHOULD ASK VICTOR TO LOOK AT THIS. IT'S HIS AREA, AFTER ALL.
I SUSPECT HE MIGHT BE BUSY, SIR.
...AFTER A CITYWIDE CATASTROPHE WAS NARROWLY AVERTED WHEN THE JUSTICE LEAGUE WATCHTOWER SATELLITE ALMOST IMPACTED SAN FRANCISCO A FEW MOMENTS AGO.

CELL PHONE VIDEO SEEMED TO INDICATE THE JUSTICE LEAGUE MAY HAVE SAVED THE CITY, BUT RIGHT NOW THEY SEEM TO BE ENGAGED IN A HEATED BATTLE WITH ONE OF THEIR OWN.
ON THE STREETS OF SAN FRANCISCO, IT'S THE JUSTICE LEAGUE VERSUS SIMON BAZ, ONE OF EARTH'S TWO GREEN LANTERNS...

SIR, ARE YOU ALL RIGHT?
I'LL LIVE.
DID YOU GET THE CODE?
I BELIEVE SO, SIR. WHAT DO YOU WANT TO DO WITH IT?
WE NEED TO FIND OUT WHO DID THIS TO US. THEY GOT PAST ALL OUR DEFENSES AND HIT US HARD AT HOME.
ONE OF YOUR MORE COLORFUL PLAYMATES, SIR?
WE'LL NEED TO DO FORENSICS ON THIS CODE TO FIND OUT.
MIGHT I SUGGEST WE DO SO UPSTAIRS?

MASTER BRUCE?
=COUGH=
SIR?
BRUCE?
HERE.
...I'M HERE...

SAN FRANCISCO WATERFRONT.
YOU WERE, WHAT, HACKED?
SOMETHING EMBEDDED IN A NEWS FEED I WAS WATCHING.
CRASHED THE SATELLITE. BROUGHT YOU HERE. NOT ME.

UNF...
...NOT... ME...
SOMEBODY STOP...ME...
VICTOR, I DON'T WANT TO HURT YOU...
DO SOMETHING NOW...BEFORE IT...

ACCESSED NEW SYSTEM. UPLOADING...
OH NO...

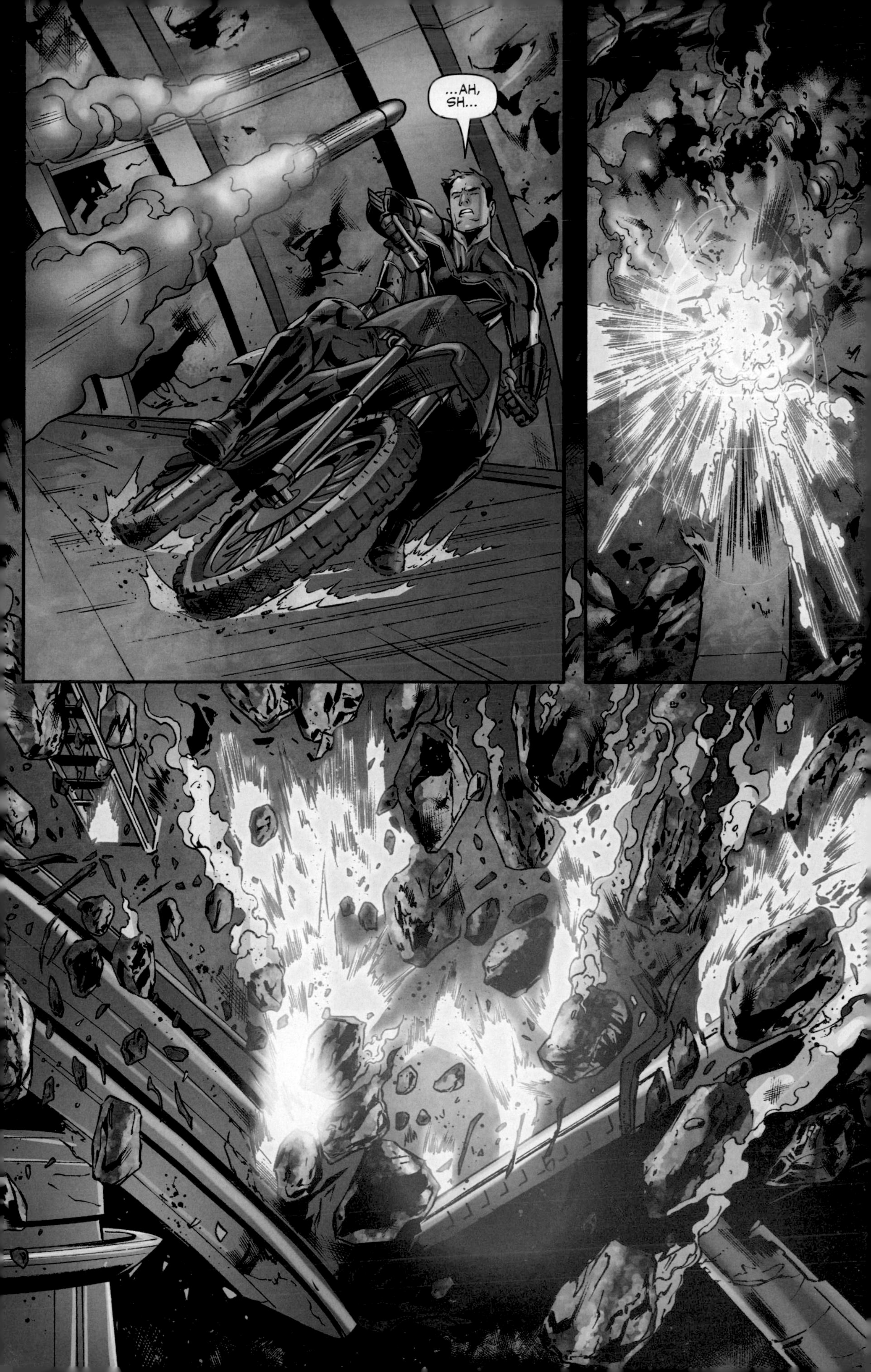
...AH, SH...

REACQUIRING PRIMARY TARGET...
NOW, ALFRED!
TARGET REACQUIRED.
IS THIS WIRELESS? WHERE DO I PLUG IT IN...?
OPERATING SYSTEM FOUND. UPLOADING.
AH-HA!
REROUTING SYSTEM...
SYSTEM UPLOAD 25%.
COME ON, COME ON. IS THIS BLOODY CLOCKWORK?
REROUTING FIRING SYSTEMS...
FIRING SYSTEM REROUTED.
UPLOAD 45% COMPLETE.
OH, FOR GOD'S SAKE...
...FIRING...
UPLOAD 100% COMPLETE.

THIS OLD BIKE IS PRE-DIGITAL. I COULD DRAW FIRE WHILE YOU GET INSIDE THE CAR. GET WHATEVER THIS VIRUS IS OUT.
GOOD PLAN. OTHER WAY AROUND.
...SEARCHING FOR TARGETS...
I FEEL LIKE I OUGHT TO SAY SOMETHING PROFOUNDLY WITTY. A QUIP TO REMEMBER THIS MOMENT BY, PERHAPS.
ALAS, I'VE GOT NOTHING.
...SECONDARY TARGET ACQUIRED...
YOU'VE GOT ME.

WE GOT YOUR DISTRESS CALL, VICTOR.
GREEN LANTERN.
WONDER WOMAN.
AQUAMAN.
FLASH.
IT WASN'T ME.
WHOEVER HACKED ME BROUGHT THEM HERE, AND CONSIDERING IT TRIED TO DROP A SATELLITE ON SAN FRANCISCO, IT PROBABLY DOESN'T HAVE OUR BEST INTERESTS IN MIND...
"JUST ONE VEHICLE LEFT..."
I'M EMPTY.
SO AM I.
I'VE GOT AN EXTERNAL DRIVE WITH A HIGH COMPRESSION ALGORITHM BUILT IN.
IT SHOULD PULL ALL THE OPERATING SYSTEMS OUT OF THE FULL NETWORK AND HOLD IT IN A CLOSED LOOP.
I NEED TO GET IN THE CAR AND MAKE A DIRECT CONNECTION TO GET WHATEVER IS CONTROLLING IT OUT.
THEN WE CAN FIND OUT WHO'S DOING THIS TO US.

...AND BACK INTO ORBIT.
WELL, ROUGHLY.
BOOOOM
ACCESS TO BOOM TUBE ACHIEVED.

SENDING OUT DISTRESS SIGNALS AND OPENING BOOM TUBES TO THIS LOCATION.
NO, NO, NO...

IT WASN'T GONE. IT JUST LET ME THINK IT WAS SO I WOULD ACCESS THE BOOM TECH. IT COULDN'T, SO IT GOT ME TO DO IT.
OW.
WHICH IS WHY I'M NOT TAKING THE EASY WAY DOWN... CAN'T BOOM.

...THIS IS GONNA HURT.

BOOM
BOOM
BOOM
BOO
OW.
BOOM TUBES OPENING...

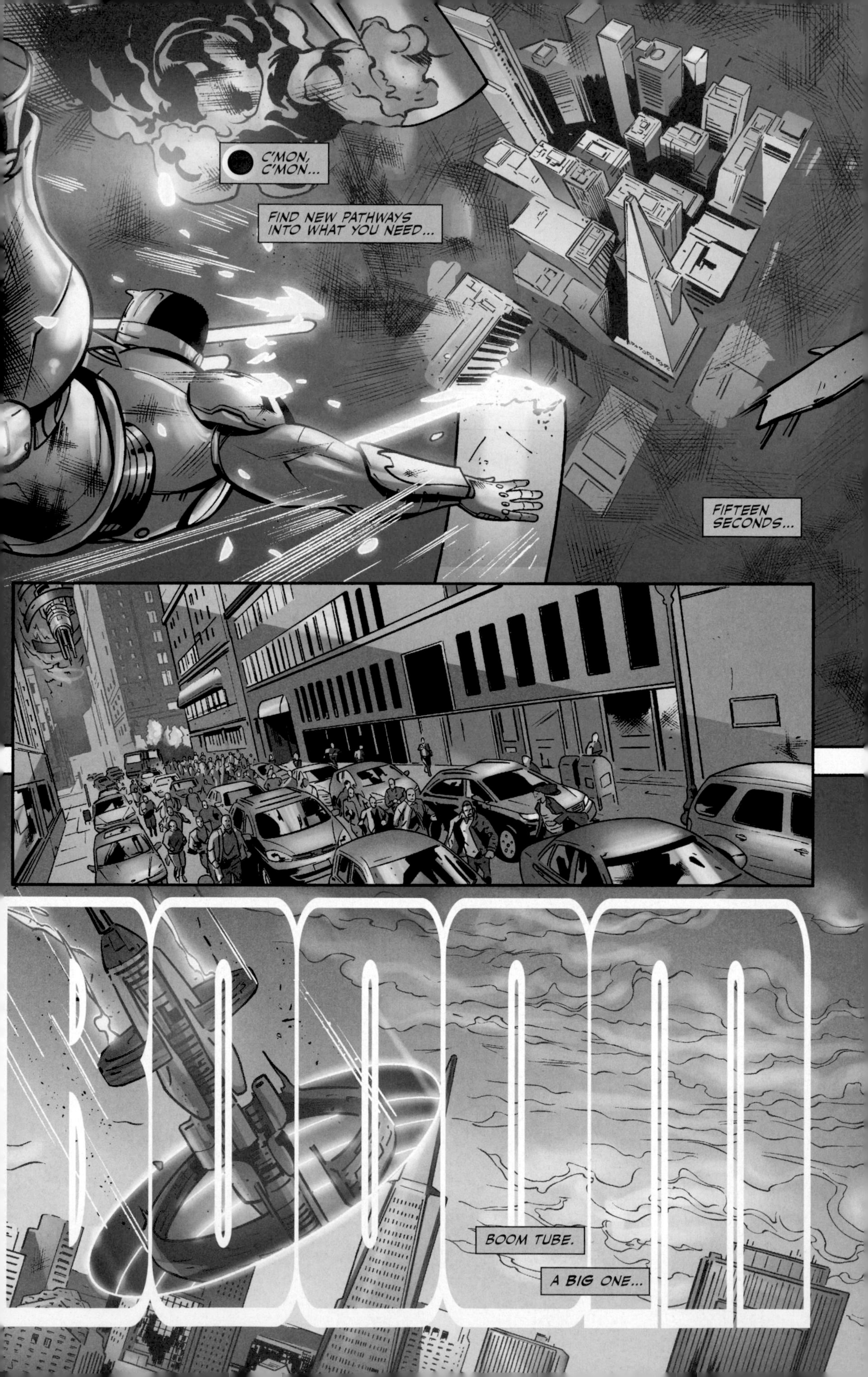
C'MON, C'MON...
FIND NEW PATHWAYS INTO WHAT YOU NEED...
FIFTEEN SECONDS...
BOOOOM
BOOM TUBE.
A BIG ONE...

"I'LL TAKE CARE OF US, NO MATTER WHAT, BOBBY.
"I'VE GOT PLANS, YOU'LL SEE."
GOT IT.

DENVER. THE HOME OF DIANE PALMER (DECEASED) AND HER FAMILY. AFTER THE FUNERAL.
"IS THE WORLD'S BANKING CRISIS SET TO RETURN?
REPORTS ARE COMING IN FROM THE WORLD'S BANKS SUGGESTING TENS OF BILLIONS OF DOLLARS' WORTH OF BONDS, ACCOUNTS AND OTHER REVENUE HAVE BEEN WIPED FROM WORLD TRADING TODAY.
MORE ON THIS STORY AND WHAT IT MEANS FOR THE AVERAGE AMERICAN, WE GET IT..."
YOU GOTTA EAT SOMETHING, BOBBY.
NOT HUNGRY.
YOU'RE NOT EATING, LILY, SO NEITHER AM I.
I GOT THINGS TO DO HERE. YOU KNOW, LAUNDRY AND STUFF.
I CAN HELP.
BETTER IF YOU PLAY. YOU CAN PLAY WITH MY IPAD ALL DAY. I GOTTA DO THE STUFF MOM DID NOW.
WHAT ABOUT DAD? HE'S BEEN IN THE GARAGE SINCE WE GOT BACK FROM, Y'KNOW, THE CEMETERY. WHAT'S HE EVEN DOING IN THERE?
HE'S, DUNNO, TRYING TO FIGURE STUFF OUT.
WHAT ABOUT US? MOM'S GONE, WHY'S HE GONE?

ROAR
IS THAT DIRECT ENOUGH FOR YOU, SIR?

ALFRED, ANYTHING?
WE'RE STILL LOCKED OUT. LOCKED IN, TOO. ALL EXITS ARE SEALED.
I'VE TRIED REWIRING AND REBOOTING THE WHOLE BLOODY SYSTEM, BUT WHATEVER THIS IS, IT WON'T BE PURGED.
NOT BY ANYTHING I CAN DO ANYWAY.
MAYBE A MORE DIRECT APPROACH?
MEANING?
YOU'RE ENGLISH, USE YOUR PIONEERING SPIRIT...
...GOT TO BE KIDDING ME...

STILL CAN'T ACCESS BOOM TUBES OR COMMS.
THAT CODE WAS REWRITING ALL MY SYSTEMS, ALL THE PATHWAYS ARE WRONG.
REROUTING... GOING TO TAKE SOME TIME...
...I'VE GOT A WATCHTOWER TO CATCH...
...GOT LESS THAN FOUR MINUTES BEFORE IT HITS SAN FRANCISCO.

...OH, THAT'S JUST GREAT...
I HAVE NO MOTOR CONTROL...
...CAN'T GRAB ON, CAN'T REACQUIRE THE WATCHTOWER SYSTEMS...
WAIT...
...GONE...
...THE CODE'S GONE.
I'M BACK ONLINE.

BOAT SYSTEMS OFFLINE.
AH!
COMPUTER, CONTACT THE OTHER MEMBERS. EMERGENCY PROTOCOLS.
UNABLE TO COMPLY. ATMOSPHERIC ENTRY IN TWENTY SECONDS.
GNNH CAN'T STOP.
WHERE'S IT TAKING ME?
IT'S INSIDE MY MOTOR SYSTEMS. TRYING TO ACCESS EVERYTHING.
FIGHT IT.
IT'S TRYING TO ACCESS BOOM TUBES AND INFORMATION ON OTHER MEMBERS. LOCK IT OUT.
NOW ENTERING ATMOSPHERE.
AIRLOCK OPEN.

SURFACE-TO-AIR MISSILES ENGAGED...
DAMN IT...
AIR-ASSAULT VEHICLE DESTROYED. BOAT SYSTEMS SEARCHING FOR TARGET...
UNF
TARGET ACQUIRED...

ALL WEAPON SYSTEMS, STAND DOWN.
UNABLE TO COMPLY.
DISENGAGE.
NEGATIVE.
DISENGAGE ALL HOSTILE PROTOCOLS. ALL WEAPONS, ALL VEHICLES. AUTHORIZATION MARTHAWAYNE1940.
AUTHORIZATION INVALID.
GNNH

ALL SAFETIES ARE DISENGAGED.
LETHAL FORCE AUTHORIZED...
NOT BY ME--!
SOMETHING IS IN THE SYSTEMS WE JUST INSTALLED... STAY HERE. THE CARS' GUNS SHOULDN'T REACH YOU.
WE SHOULD GO UPSTAIRS. NOTHING TO SHOOT AT IF WE LEAVE THE CAVE.
YOU GO. IF IT'S IN ALL THE VEHICLE SYSTEMS, THEN THEY MIGHT GET OUT.
THEY'RE ALMOST ALL FULLY AUTONOMOUS. IMAGINE THE DAMAGE THEY COULD DO.
AH.

PERHAPS I COULD INTEREST YOU IN A SANDWICH BEFORE YOU GO OUT AND STRIKE FEAR INTO THE COWARDLY CRIMINAL FRATERNITY. SIR?
P.B. AND J.?
JUST LEAVE IT IN THE KITCHEN, ALFRED. FOR WHEN I GET *BACK.*
ACCESSING ALL VEHICLE SCHEMATICS...

SIR, I THINK WE'RE BEING *HACKED!*
NOTHING SHOULD BE ABLE TO GET THROUGH *THESE* FIREWALLS...

"...NOT EVEN VICTOR."
IT'S IN ME...
THE CODE JUMPED WITH THE PHOTONS IN MY OCULAR RECEPTORS.
IT'S IN THE WATCHTOWER...
...THROUGH ME, MY CONNECTION, IT'S IN THE WATCHTOWER SYSTEMS...
ACCESSING SATELLITE SYSTEMS. ORBITAL ADJUSTMENT THRUSTERS ENGAGED. ATMOSPHERIC ENTRY IN THREE MINUTES.

ACCESSING VEHICLE SYSTEMS. TARGETS IDENTIFIED...
ALFRED, GET OUT!
NOW!
SIR...?

INITIATING SOFTWARE UPGRADES FOR ALL VEHICLES.
IT WAS WAR, ALFRED. THE MIRACLE WAS THAT THE CASUALTY LIST WASN'T IN THE THOUSANDS OR WORSE.
WHEN THERE ARE BEINGS THAT CAN BRING DOWN OUR CITIES OR TEAR OUR WORLD IN HALF, WE HOLD THE LINE.
THERE ISN'T A SINGLE ONE OF US WHO WOULDN'T HAVE GIVEN HIS OR HER OWN LIFE TO STOP WHAT HAPPENED TO DIANE PALMER.
SOMETIMES, EVEN ON YOUR BEST DAYS, IT'S JUST NOT ENOUGH.
WHAT IS THAT?
I CAN HEAR SOMETHING. LIKE A BACKGROUND NOISE IN THE LIVE FEED.
NO, NOT A BACKGROUND NOISE...
...IT'S MORE LIKE A FOREGROUND IMAGE.
IT'S SOME SORT OF CODE.
NEVER SEEN CODE LIKE THAT BEFORE AND IT'S HIDDEN IN THE PHOTONS.
WHAT'S IT DOING IN THE NEWS FEED...?

"...THE WORLD WATCHED AS THE JUSTICE LEAGUE FOUGHT TO SAVE THE EARTH DURING RECENT ATTACKS FROM BEINGS CALLED THE KINDRED AND THE MASSIVE SEISMIC ACTIVITY CAUSED BY THE DEVICES WE NOW KNOW WERE HIDDEN IN OUR PLANET'S CORE."
"THE WORLD WATCHES TODAY AS DIANE PALMER IS LAID TO REST BY HER SURVIVING FAMILY."
"IT IS BECAUSE OF THE JUSTICE LEAGUE THAT, DESPITE THE LARGE NUMBER OF INJURED WORLDWIDE, THERE HAS ONLY BEEN A SINGLE FATALITY."
"THAT FACT IS DOUBTLESS OF LITTLE COMFORT TO HER FAMILY TODAY."
MULTI-VEHICLE AUTONOMOUS SOFTWARE READY TO UPLOAD.
YES/NO?
BATMAN.
THAT'S ALL OF THE HARDWARE REPAIRS NEEDED AFTER SUPERMAN'S..."VISIT." IF WE GET ANY OTHER VISITORS, WE SHOULD HAVE SOMETHING TO GREET THEM WITH.
YOU CAN INITIATE ALL THE SECURITY SOFTWARE UPGRADES NOW, ALFRED.
CERTAINLY, MASTER BRUCE.
TRAGIC, ISN'T IT, SIR?

OUTBREAK PART ONE

BRYAN HITCH WRITER / NEIL EDWARDS PENCILLER / DANIEL HENRIQUES INKER
TONY AVIÑA COLORIST / RICHARD STARKINGS & COMICRAFT LETTERING
FERNANDO PASARIN, MATT RYAN & BRAD ANDERSON COVER
YANICK PAQUETTE & NATHAN FAIRBAIRN VARIANT COVER
AMEDEO TURTURRO & DIEGO LOPEZ ASSISTANT EDITORS / BRIAN CUNNINGHAM EDITOR

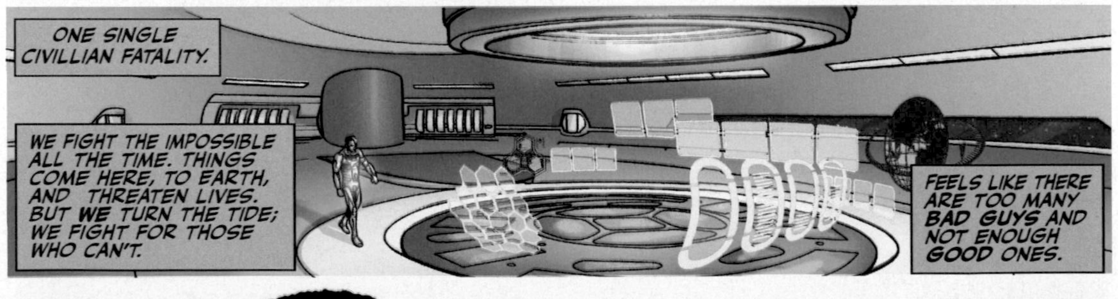

SEATTLE.
GLAD YOU CALLED, JESS. HOPING YOU WOULD.
YOU OKAY?
I HAVEN'T TOLD SIMON YET BUT I WANT YOU TO TELL THE OTHERS, I'M LEAVING.
LEAVING? LEAVING WHAT?
THE TEAM. THE LEAGUE.
I'LL CARRY ON BEING A GREEN LANTERN BUT I DON'T WANT TO BE IN THE LEAGUE. NOT RIGHT NOW AND NOT AFTER...YOU KNOW.
AFTER.
THAT WASN'T ME, JESS. NOT US. NOT REALLY. YOU HAVE TO BELIEVE THAT.
IT WAS. MAYBE. JUST A LITTLE BIT.

I FELT ALL OF IT. ALL OF YOU, ALL OF THE OTHERS. NOT JUST THE BITS YOU ALL LET OUT BUT ALSO ALL OF THE BITS YOU DIDN'T. EVERYTHING THAT CREATURE FELT WENT THROUGH ME.
I CAN'T BE AROUND THAT. AROUND ALL OF YOU.
IT'S MADE ME THINK I'M NOT READY.

AND FOR US? BECAUSE REALLY, I THINK...
FOR THE LEAGUE.
COME ON, PLEASE DON'T DO THIS. WE NEED YOU.
NO, YOU DON'T. THIS WAS HAL'S CHOICE AND NOW I'M MAKING MINE.

YOU'LL TELL THE OTHERS?
IF THAT'S REALLY WHAT YOU WANT.
IT IS. RIGHT NOW, IT IS.

YOU AND ME?
TAKE IT SLOW, BARRY ALLEN.
TAKE IT SLOW.

SSSH JESS. YOU WERE AMAZING. IT'S GOING TO BE OKAY...
IT'S GOING TO BE FINE.
NO, IT ISN'T. I CAN STILL FEEL EVERYBODY. FADING BUT STILL THERE...

"...THAT THING DIDN'T MAKE US FEEL THESE THINGS, THEY WERE ALL THERE ALREADY.
"IT JUST MADE US SEE THEM."

"UNDER ALL THOSE COSTUMES, WE'RE STILL PEOPLE, JESS. THAT'S NOTHING TO BE AFRAID OF."
"IT'S NOT ALL COSTUMES, BARRY, AND THERE'S PLENTY TO FEAR FOR ALL OF US.
"I FELT OTHER STUFF FROM THAT THING. NOTHING I CAN PUT A SHAPE TO BUT SOMETHING BIG. TERRIBLE."

"WE'RE TIGHT, OKAY? WE'RE THE JUSTICE LEAGUE."
"NOT THE SAME ONE YOU WERE. NOT THE SAME PEOPLE.
"ALL OF THIS, ALL WE'VE FELT HERE...

"...THERE'S GOING TO BE CONSEQUENCES."

SHOW US YOUR LIGHT, JESSICA...
SHOW EVERYONE.

YOU CAN'T EVER TRULY SEND ME AWAY. I'M AN INFECTION, A CANCER THAT WILL GROW IN YOU, ALL OF YOU.
FEAR IS JUST THE BEGINNING.
NO!
GAAAAAAAAAA!

RIGHT LANE MUST EXIT

MY INFECTION JUST TOUCHES THE SURFACE. IT ASKS YOU TO LOOK DEEPER INTO YOURSELVES. WHAT WILL YOU FIND?
HOW TOGETHER ARE YOU? HOW UNITED?
YOU AREN'T.
BARRY?
...HERE, I THINK. HARD TO FOCUS ON A *SINGLE* MOMENT...
...EACH ONE AN AGE...
...HARD TO BE *HERE.*

GRAB MY *HAND.* FIND IT. FOCUS ON THAT!

...GOT IT!
HOLD ON, BARRY, HOLD ON...

HEY...YOU! *THING.* WHATEVER YOU ARE, WHEREVER YOU *CAME* FROM.
YOU'RE THE DARK CORNERS, THE HIDDEN UGLINESS. THE PARTS WE DON'T *WANT* OTHERS TO SEE.
I SEE FEAR IN YOU MORE THAN THE OTHERS. THEIR ANGER, ISOLATION, SELF-LOATHING AND GUILT.
YOU WANT TO HIDE FROM ALL OF THEM IN CASE THEY SEE YOUR TRUE FEARS. YOUR FEAR OF THEM...

JESSICA, BEING A GREEN LANTERN ISN'T ABOUT *NOT* BEING AFRAID, IT'S ABOUT OVERCOMING *FEAR.*
WE'RE ALL AFRAID OF SOMETHING, *LOADS* OF THINGS. BUT IT CAN'T *DEFINE* US...

MY PARENTS DIED, TOO, YOU KNOW.
THEY SAVED YOU, SENT YOU HERE. AN ACT OF HOPE, OF LOVE. NOT SENSELESS VIOLENCE.
YOU GOT NEW PARENTS WHO SHOWED YOU WHAT IT IS TO BE A GOOD PERSON.
WE AREN'T THE SAME.
WE DON'T HAVE TO BE.
I HAD TO CONTROL MY FEELINGS, TOO, EVEN AS A CHILD. ANGER, RAGE, CONFUSION. ANYTHING THAT MEANT I COULDN'T CONTROL MY STRENGTH AND POWER.
I WAS ANGRY WITH LOIS, SHE WAS ANGRY WITH ME. WE'RE NEVER LIKE THAT. IT WAS HORRIBLE.
I WANT TO TEAR YOU APART.
YOU'VE MADE ME ANGRIER THAN I'VE EVER FELT.
HAVE I?
IS IT REALLY ME?

"OR IS IT SOMETHING ELSE?"
I AM JUST A BREATH, A THOUGHT.
A QUESTION.
WHAT DO YOU FEAR ABOUT YOURSELVES?

JESSICA?
BARRY?
YOU CAN HEAR ME?
YEAH. NOT HEAR, MORE LIKE I CAN **FEEL** WHAT YOU'RE SAYING...
...WHAT YOU'RE FEELING.
...GOING ON? ...THAT THING WE JUST BEAT...?
...DIDN'T. IT WAS IN ME, THROUGH THE RING, WE'RE ALL CONNECTED...
...GOT TO **ALL** OF US...

...CAN FEEL THE REST OF THEM... THE LEAGUE...
...IT'S HORRIBLE, BARRY... LIKE A WOUND FOR EACH OF US...
...BARRY...?
...BARRY...?

I **REALLY** WANT TO KILL YOU.
I WOULD LET YOU.
I'VE SPENT MY LIFE **CONTROLLING** MY FEELINGS, MY GUILT. ENOUGH TO KNOW THIS ISN'T NORMAL. FOR EITHER OF US.
RIGHT NOW I FEEL LIKE I DESERVE YOUR ANGER. LIKE I WANT IT.

I'VE ALWAYS BEEN **AFRAID** MY GUILT WOULD **CONTROL** ME. IF IT DID, I WOULDN'T BE ABLE TO DO THIS ANYMORE.
I SURVIVED WHEN MY PARENTS DIDN'T. WHEN JASON DIDN'T.
I'VE FELT GUILTY FOR EVERY LIFE THE JOKER TOOK WHEN I SHOULD HAVE BROKEN HIS NECK A LONG TIME AGO.
MAYBE ONE DAY I **WILL.**

SAN DIEGO NAVAL BASE.
WHAT SORT OF THREAT DO YOU THINK YOU ARE?
TELL YOUR PRESIDENT I'VE BROUGHT HIS WAR TOYS BACK.
TELL HIM HE WILL SEE MY OWN IF HE DOESN'T KEEP HIS WEAPONS OF MASS DESTRUCTION OFF MY SHORES.
I'M TAKING THIS MESSAGE TO THE RUSSIANS NEXT. TO EVERYONE.

TELL HIM THAT PEACE IS COMING.

WHAT HAPPENS WHEN PEOPLE WITH THE POWER TO CHANGE WORLDS ARE GOVERNED BY THEIR FEARS?
HOW PROTECTED WILL THIS WORLD BE THEN?
WHEN I PLAGUE THIS PLANET AND ITS PEOPLES, WHO THEN WILL STAND AGAINST WHAT IS COMING TO CLAIM YOU ALL?
FEAR LEADS TO HATRED, CONFLICT, WAR.
WHERE ARE THE HEROES WHEN THEY BECOME THE HUNTED?
BULLETS?
SERIOUSLY?

NOT GONE. THROUGH YOUR RING, INFECTED YOU.
THERE'S NOWHERE TO RUN TO. I'M INSIDE
ISOLATION AND SELF-LOATHING.
HE FEARS HE DOESN'T BELONG WITH THE REST OF YOU, THE CORPS, HIS COMMUNITY, HIS FAITH. HE BELONGS NOWHERE.
HE MAKES HIS FEARS REAL. ALL DO.
THIS ONE ALREADY FELT APART. DIFFERENT. NOW HIS FEARS ABOUT HIS DISFIGUREMENT MAKE HIM LOATHE HIMSELF.
HE'S A MONSTER. A VICTIM.
HE FEARS IT, SO IT IS. THAT FEAR INFECTS ALL THOSE AROUND HIM. IF THAT'S HOW HE DEFINES HIMSELF, THEN THAT'S HOW OTHERS WILL DEFINE HIM, TOO.

IS THAT JESS I CAN HEAR? VOICES...
NOT HEAR, NOT AT THIS SPEED. FEEL. I CAN FEEL VOICES...
JESS, CAN YOU HEAR THAT...?
GET AWAY FROM ME, BARRY!
GOING TO BE SICK...

HUWAARRGGHH!
FEED ON IT.

IT WAS SUPPOSED TO BE A DATE FOR JESS AND ME.
PROBABLY FOR ALL THESE FOLKS, TOO.
WENT TOO FAST AND BLEW IT FOR ALL OF US. SCARED HER.
I'M AN IDIOT.

I CAN FIND OUT EVERYTHING ABOUT ALL OF THESE PEOPLE BEFORE THEY'D BLINK. CHECK WALLETS FOR ADDRESSES, GO TO THEIR HOMES AND GO THROUGH THEIR LIVES.
ALL BETWEEN THE PAUSES IN THEIR HEARTBEATS.

BEING THIS FAST MEANS I COULD CHANGE THE WORLD, TRULY CHANGE IT FOR EVERYBODY, BUT NEVER LIVE IN IT.
EVERY BREATH PEOPLE TAKE IS A LIFETIME FOR ME. ALONE.
SO I SLOW DOWN. JOIN THE WORLD. IGNORE MY TRUE POTENTIAL AND SAY IT'S FOR THE RIGHT REASONS.

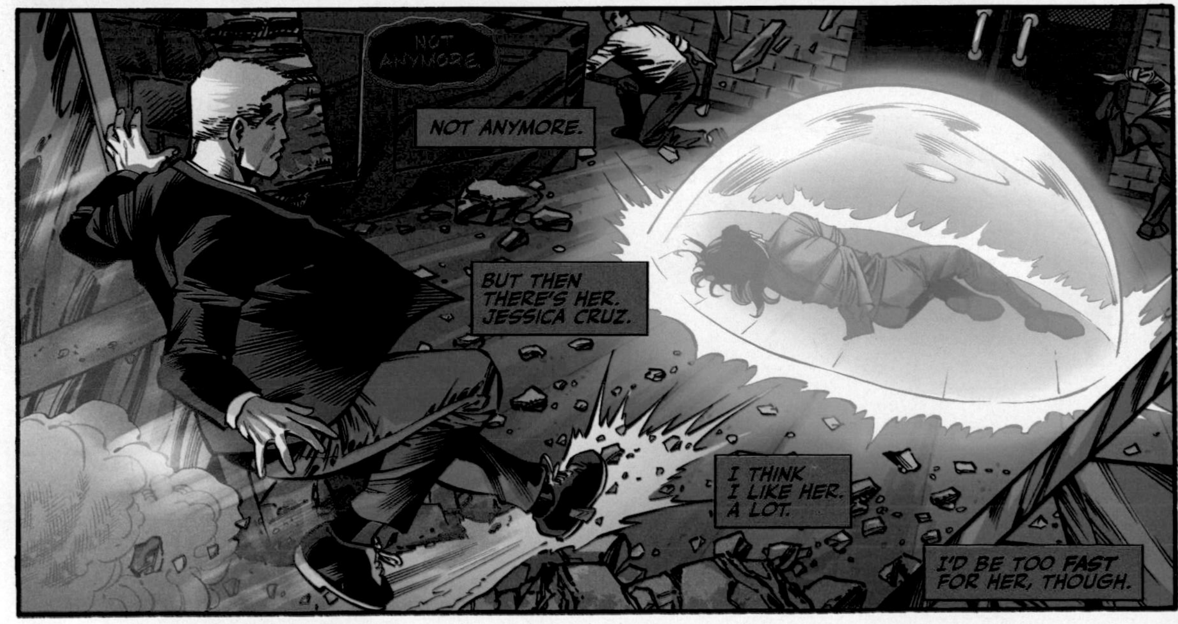
NOT ANYMORE.
NOT ANYMORE.
BUT THEN THERE'S HER. JESSICA CRUZ.
I THINK I LIKE HER. A LOT.
I'D BE TOO FAST FOR HER, THOUGH.

SO WE ALL GOING TO GRAB A BURGER... AND...

THEY'RE LOOKING AT ME.
EVERYONE'S LOOKING AT ME.

DON'T LOOK AT ME! GET AWAY, DON'T LOOK!
VIC? MAN, WHAT'RE YOU DOING...?
DON'T LOOK AT ME!

I DON'T THINK I'VE EVER BELONGED ANYWHERE.
DEFINITELY NOT THE LEAGUE. THEY DON'T WANT ME.

GOT TO HIDE.
CAN'T LET ANYONE SEE ME.

NOBODY WANTS ME AROUND.

OH MY GOD, DID YOU SEE THAT...?
...GET AWAY...
...THAT CYBORG THING...
...HIDEOUS...
...HIDE...

DETRO MICHIGAN. FORD HIGH SCHOOL.
TOUCHDOWN, CROWD GOES *WILD!*
IT'S GOING WILD, RIGHT?
RIGHT!
WHERE WAS YOUR *DEFENSE,* GUYS? GOT PAST YOU LIKE YOU WEREN'T THERE!
CHEATING, DUDE. EVERY TIME WITH THOSE *BOOM* THINGS OF YOURS!
I SUPPOSE WE SHOULD BE HAPPY YOU DON'T BRING FLASH TO THESE GAMES.
OR BATMAN.

WHY DID I LET CYBORG BRING ME HERE?
I DON'T *BELONG* HERE LIKE HE DOES. SHOULD HAVE JUST GONE HOME, SIMON.

JUST BE LEFT ALONE.

WE *PROTECT* THE PEOPLE OF THIS WORLD BUT WE DON'T *CHANGE* THEM.
WE LET GOVERNMENTS ARGUE SOVEREIGNTY, RELIGIONS ARGUE MORALITY, WHEN *WE* ARE THE TRUE SUPER-POWERS IN THE WORLD.
I RULE ONE OF THE LARGEST NATIONS ON THE PLANET. I'VE TRIED TO BE TOLERANT, BUT THEY ARE MAKING THAT DIFFICULT.
PRESIDENTS CHANGE. GOVERNMENTS CHANGE. POLICIES CHANGE. WHAT WOULD HAPPEN IF *WE* TOOK CHARGE?
WE COULD *MAKE* A BETTER WORLD.
THEY HAVE VESSELS EQUIPPED WITH ENOUGH NUCLEAR WEAPONS TO DESTROY *HALF* THE WORLD RESTING BENEATH *MY* WATERS AND ABOVE MY CITIES. I'M TERRIFIED FOR MY PEOPLE.

I'M A PRINCESS, YOU'RE A KING.
MAYBE IT'S TIME TO MAKE AN *OFFICIAL* STATEMENT?
THEY'VE MADE ME TRULY AFRAID TO TRUST THEM.
I THINK THE TIME FOR WORDS HAS PASSED.

I'M GOING TO SHOW AMERICA HOW *SMALL* IT IS.

THE U.S. ATLANTIC COAST.
THEY THINK I'M A TERRORIST NOW.
I'VE BEEN RIDICULED, BEEN A HERO. NOW I'M FEARED AND HATED, WONDER WOMAN.
I CAME HERE ON A MISSION OF PEACE.
I'M STARTING TO THINK THE ONLY WAY I COULD ACHIEVE THAT WOULD BE TO CONQUER THE WHOLE WORLD, AQUAMAN.
I'M AFRAID OF WHAT THAT COULD MEAN.
I PULL THESE WRECKS OUT FROM TIME TO TIME. THE SURFACE WORLD LITTERS MY WORLD WITH THEIR WEAPONS OF WAR AND THEY CALL ME A TERRORIST?
IF I'D WANTED IT TO, ATLANTIS COULD HAVE SHOWN THEM THE MEANING OF THE WORD. IF I GIVE IN TO MY FEAR, I COULD START A WAR.

I'VE DONE EVERYTHING YOU'VE ASKED.
EVERYTHING!
I'LL KEEP DOING IT, KEEP SAVING THE WORLD, YOU KNOW THAT. AND IF I DO DIE? WHO LOOKS AFTER JON AND LOIS THEN?
YOU?
YOU'VE DONE SOMETHING NO BAD GUY EVER REALLY DID.
YOU'VE PISSED ME OFF.

YOU ASKED ME TO GO TO THE EARTH'S CORE.
YOU ASKED ME AND I DID IT. EVEN AFTER ALMOST DYING, LEAVING MY WIFE AND SON ON YOUR SAY-SO, YOU STILL DON'T TRUST ME.
HOW MANY MORE TIMES?
GNH!

WE'RE ALL AFRAID OF SOMETHING.
HOW MANY SHOULD I HAVE SAVED IN MY WAR ON CRIME BUT DIDN'T?
IT STARTED WITH MY PARENTS. I WATCHED AS THEY WERE SHOT AND I DID NOTHING. NOT THEN. NOT FOR YEARS.
JASON TODD? HE WAS A CHILD. THE JOKER KILLED HIM, BUT IT WAS MY FAULT I DIDN'T SAVE HIM.
STATE OF FEAR PART TWO
BRYAN HITCH WRITER
JESUS MERINO PENCILLER
ANDY OWENS INKER
ADRIANO LUCAS COLORIST
RICHARD STARKINGS + COMICRAFT LETTERING
TONY S. DANIEL + SANDU FLOREA COVER
YANICK PAQUETTE + NATHAN FAIRBAIRN VARIANT COVER
AMEDEO TURTURRO + DIEGO LOPEZ ASSISTANT EDITORS
BRIAN CUNNINGHAM EDITOR

FATHER, MENTOR, PARTNER. BRUCE OR BATMAN, IN THE END I'M AS GUILTY AS THOSE I FIGHT.
AND MY PUNISHMENT IS COMING.

Tony S Daniel 2016 & FLOREA

Tony S. Daniel 2016
& FLOREA

YOU NOT EATING, CLARK? I THOUGHT YOU WERE STARVING.
I'M NOT HUNGRY.
HEADACHE.

YOU HAVEN'T BEEN YOURSELF SINCE YOU GOT BACK FROM THE EARTH'S CORE LAST WEEK.
BATMAN SAID--
DON'T TALK TO ME ABOUT BATMAN.

BATMAN. THIS ALL STARTED GOING WRONG WHEN HE SHOWED UP.
HE DOESN'T TRUST ME, SO HE'S POISONING YOUR MIND AGAINST ME.
DON'T BE STUPID. YOU'RE SO DESPERATE FOR HIM TO APPROVE OF YOU THAT YOU'RE WILLING TO THROW EVERYTHING AWAY WHEN HE SNAPS HIS FINGERS.

I'M GOING TO SEE HIM. HE CAN'T COME HERE AND SCREW UP MY LIFE, OUR LIVES, LIKE THIS.
WHAT ARE YOU GOING TO DO? ASK HIM TO GIVE YOU A PAT ON THE BACK?
CALL YOU AN INSPIRATION?

DO? I'M GOING TO KILL HIM.

HIDE.
DON'T GO OUT.

SAFE.
BE SAFE.

SHOULD GO HOME. HOME IS SAFE.
CAN'T LEAVE HERE. CAN'T GO OUTSIDE.

SAFE HERE.
JESSICA, YOU IN HERE?

C'MON, LET'S BLOW THIS JOINT...

UNNN...

MADAM, YOU'RE CAUSING A SCENE, PLEASE CALM--
DON'T.

DON'T LET HIM TOUCH YOU.

I DIDN'T MEAN TO...
I THOUGHT HE WAS GOING TO TOUCH ME...
YOU ASK ME, HE DESERVED THAT. HE WAS LOOKING AT YOU FUNNY.
THEY ALL ARE. I MEAN, YOU ARE MAKING A FUSS. CAN'T YOU JUST CALM DOWN?

GET AWAY. RUN AWAY.
HIDE...
WHY...WHY WOULD YOU SAY THAT?

HEY, WHERE YOU GOING?
DON'T LET ALL THIS SLOWNESS SPOIL OUR DATE...

ANY OF YOU LOOKING DOWN YOUR NOSES AT US MIGHT WANT TO REMEMBER WE'VE SAVED YOUR LITTLE LIVES MORE TIMES THAN ANY OF YOU DESERVE.
YOU'RE WELCOME.

DO YOU REALLY EAT THAT MUCH?
MORE, ACTUALLY, BUT I DIDN'T WANT TO LOOK GREEDY IN FRONT OF A LADY.
I DON'T DATE MUCH.
I MUST HAVE HAD A DATE, Y'KNOW, SOMETIME.
I JUST CAN'T REMEMBER WHEN THAT WAS. MIGHT HAVE BEEN HIGH SCHOOL.

COULD WE, LIKE, MOVE THINGS ALONG A BIT FASTER?
THE SERVICE HERE IS *REALLY* SLOW.
BARRY, WE JUST ORDERED. DON'T HAVE TO RUSH EVERYTHING, RIGHT?

FEELS LIKE I'VE BEEN IN HERE FOR *DAYS.*
ALL THE TIME I HAVE TO SLOW DOWN. I'M NOT OUT THERE SAVING FOLKS... LIKE MY MOM.
OH NO, I'M SORRY. I KNEW I SHOULDN'T HAVE ASKED YOU OUT. I SHOULD GO.
I'M GETTING SCARED AGAIN...
LIKE IT USED TO BE...

NO, NO, NO, NO. HE'S TOUCHING ME...
HEY, JESS, YOU OKAY?
I CAN'T, HE...CAN'T...

GET *OFF* ME!
DON'T *TOUCH* ME!

RISTORANTE DORIA, SEATTLE, WASHINGTON.
SEEMS NICE HERE.
YEAH. MENU LOOKS GOOD.
YOU LOOK NICE, TOO.
THANKS, YOU THINK SO? I'M BEGINNING TO THINK GREEN MIGHT BE MY COLOR.

HOW'S ALL THAT GOING FOR YOU?
THE RING? OKAY. GETTING THERE ANYWAY, I THINK.
SEEM PRETTY HANDY IN THE FIELD.

SIMON'S MUCH BETTER AT THE HARDWARE THAN I AM. HE'S A NATURAL.
I'M... WELL, I DON'T KNOW WHAT I AM.
HUNGRY?
VERY.

READY TO ORDER, SIR, MADAM?
LADIES FIRST.
OH, OKAY. WELL, CAN I HAVE JUST THE SALAD TO START AND THEN THE SEA BASS, PLEASE?
CERTAINLY, MADAM. AND SIR?

CAN I GET THE SALAD, TOO, PLEASE, BUT WITH EXTRA CHICKEN, AND THE BREAD BASKET WITH GNOCCHI TO START?
AAAAND I'LL HAVE THE POLLO LINGUINE, SPAGHETTI CARBONARA AND THE RIGATONI ALLA RAGU FOR MAIN. MAYBE SOME MORE BREAD.
SIR?
I'M ON A CALORIE-CONTROLLED DIET.
YES, SIR.

"CALL DICK GRAYSON."

CALLING DICK GRAYSON...
CALLING DICK GRAYSON...
UNAVAILABLE MESSAGE. WOULD YOU LIKE TO CALL BACK?
NO.

MASTER BRUCE. I THOUGHT I HEARD YOU RETURN.
AM I INTERRUPTING, SIR? WERE YOU MAKING A PHONE CALL?
NOT REALLY.
JUST DICK. HE WASN'T THERE.

AH, MASTER DICK. I SPOKE TO HIM A FEW DAYS AGO AND HE SEEMED IN EXCELLENT SPIRITS.

I WOULDN'T KNOW, WE HAVEN'T SPOKEN.
...IS THERE ANYTHING ELSE, SIR?
I'D LIKE TO BE ALONE.

WOULD YOU, SIR?

OKAY. GOT CHANGED AGAIN. LAST TIME.
SHE'S HERE. COOL.
SHOULD'VE BROUGHT FLOWERS.

HE'S LEAVING. OHMIGOD HE'S GOING!
HE SAW ME COMING AND HE'S GOING!

WHAT DO I DO? GO HOME?
WHY WOULD HE--
JESS?

BARRY! I THOUGHT YOU'D...
LEFT?
YEAH.
NO, I JUST, WHEN I SAW YOU COMING I...
...CHANGED YOUR MIND...?
NO. I GOT FLOWERS...
THOUGHT YOU'D GONE...WAIT, FLOWERS?
YEAH. FOR YOU.
FLOWERS FOR ME...?

HERE.
OH.
SORRY, I...
...RAN TOO FAST.
THAT'S SO SWEET!
SHOULD WE MAYBE GO IN?

7:45 P.M.
EIGHT MUGGINGS IN THREE CITIES, AN ARMED ROBBERY NEAR MICHIGAN AND TWO MISSING-PERSONS CASES.
STILL TIME FOR A SHOWER IN CENTRAL CITY BEFORE HEADING TO SEATTLE.
DINNER WITH JESS. DIDN'T SEE THAT COMING.
KINDA COOL.
BARRY'S APARTMENT, CENTRAL CITY.
NICE LONG SHOWER.
MUCH BETTER.
7:46 P.M.
RISTORANTE DORIA, SEATTLE, WASHINGTON.
RISTORANTE DORIA
7:47 P.M.
I FEEL OVERDRESSED.
JESS IS A FRIEND, DON'T WANT TO COME ON STRONG.
CASUAL. BETTER...
...MAYBE NOT.
7:48 P.M.

...HE LIKES RED. MAYBE I SHOULD WEAR THE RED DRESS...?
BIT SLUTTY... YELLOW?
I SHOULD CANCEL.

WHAT WAS I THINKING? GOING ON A DATE. WITH BARRY?
I'M AN IDIOT.
I SHOULDN'T HAVE ASKED HIM. IS IT TOO LATE TO CANCEL? I COULD JUST STAY HOME AND ORDER IN NOODLES.
MAYBE WATCH LOVE ISLAND OR FRIENDS RERUNS.

I DON'T ACTUALLY HAVE BARRY'S NUMBER. NEVER THOUGHT TO ASK FOR IT.
I COULD CALL THE WATCHTOWER, I COULD SAY SOMETHING CAME UP.
AN ALIEN INVASION OR SOMETHING.
I'LL CALL SIMON.

WHAT ARE YOU DOING, JESSICA? TALKING YOURSELF OUT OF SOMETHING THAT MIGHT BE FUN?
IT'S OKAY, IT'S FINE. WE'RE FRIENDS. JUST FRIENDS HAVING DINNER.
I MEAN, NOTHING'S GOING TO HAPPEN, RIGHT?

I'M GOING TO FLOSS AGAIN.

THE KENT FARM. UPSTATE FROM METROPOLIS.
CK LL

WE SAW IT ON THE NEWS. LOOKED BAD FOR A WHILE THERE. YOU OKAY?
YEAH. BIT OF A HEADACHE. ONCE THE LANTERNS BROKE ITS HOLD WE COULD FINISH IT OFF.

WHAT WAS IT?
DON'T KNOW. BUT IT MADE US ALL FEEL AFRAID--GENUINELY AFRAID. IT'S GONE NOW ANYWAY.
THERE'LL BE SOMETHING *NEW* TOMORROW. ALWAYS IS.

HEY, WAIT UNTIL DINNER!
YOU KNOW I CAN'T PROTECT YOU AND JON ON AN EMPTY STOMACH, LOIS...

BATMAN WAS THERE. WE DIDN'T SPEAK.
SHOULD HAVE TOLD HIM HOW I FELT. I KNOW HE STILL DOESN'T TRUST ME.
LET IT GO, CLARK. HE'LL GET THERE. IF HE DOESN'T, WHAT CAN YOU DO?
DINNER IN TEN.

HI, DAD. YOU GUYS WERE *AWESOME.*
LOVE *YOU,* TOO, KIDDO.
M6

I'M IN SEATTLE. ITALIAN? THAI? BURGER? YOU'RE NOT A VEGAN OR ANYTHING, ARE YOU?
WHATEVER MAKES YOU COMFORTABLE. I'LL EAT ANYTHING, JESS. LOTS OF IT.
RISTORANTE DORIA? AT EIGHT?

IT'S A DATE!
OH MY GOD.
ZOOM

SO LOOK, I GOT THIS GAME WITH MY OLD HIGH SCHOOL FOOTBALL TEAM. YOU WANT TO COME?
FOOTBALL'S NOT REALLY MY THING.
IT'S MORE ABOUT SPENDING TIME WITH THE KIDS. IT'LL BE FUN. BURGERS AND SODA AFTER?

SURE. OKAY.

I WON'T HAVE TO PLAY, WILL I?

...WONDERING IF YOU CAN HELP ME WITH SOMETHING.
OF COURSE.

HEADING OFF?
WELL, YEAH. I GUESS. THINGS TO DO.
IS DINNER ONE OF THEM? 'CAUSE IF IT IS, I'M, Y'KNOW, FREE, TOO...?

WOW, OKAY. YOU ASKING ME ON A DATE?
I THINK SO--YEAH. ARE YOU GOING TO SAY NO?
NO, I...
OH MY GOD, YOU ARE SAYING NO. I FEEL LIKE A COMPLETE IDIOT.

NO. I MEAN, YES. I MEAN, I'M NOT SAYING NO.
REALLY?
REALLY.
WE'RE NOT ASKING THEM, TOO, RIGHT?
OH GOD, NO!
WAIT, DO YOU THINK WE SHOULD?

DEFINITELY NOT, JESS. AS FUN AS THIS ALL WOULD BE TO WATCH.
GOT OTHER PLANS. AND SO DOES HE.
I DO?
SURE YOU DO. C'MON.

EMERGENCY SERVICES ARE INBOUND TO ALL AREAS.
STARTING TO SOUND LIKE NO FATALITIES. LIMITED INJURY AND PROPERTY DAMAGE.
WE WERE LUCKY.
NEVER FELT FEAR LIKE THAT. IT WAS...
TERRIFYING.

OUR TWO ROOKIE LANTERNS WERE AMAZING. WITHOUT YOU TWO THIS COULD HAVE GONE VERY DIFFERENTLY.
THANK YOU. JUST DOING OUR JOB.
DID YOU GUYS SEE HER? "NOT TODAY!"
AWESOME. TOTALLY.
BARRY...
CAN WE TALK?
IT'LL HAVE TO BE LATER. FAMILY DINNER.

BOOM TUBES HOME FOR THOSE WHO WANT THEM.

...AND DON'T BE AFRAID.

WE'RE GREEN LANTERNS, FILTH!
FEAR WAS THE FIRST THING WE HAD TO BEAT!

=GNH= STILL NOT ENOUGH. WE'RE HOLDING IT, NOT BEATING IT.
DON'T SEE ANY...=HNN=...MORE LANTERNS...

NO, BUT THERE'S US...
EVERYONE, MAKE A LINE!

TOGETHER...
GRAB HOLD, FORM A CHAIN TO BOTH OF THEM...
EVERYONE, TAKE HANDS...

NOT TODAY!

=GNNNH= TOO MUCH... CAN'T...
SIMON!
BAZ! I NEED YOU!

...THING'S *MAKING* US ALL *AFRAID.* TOO AFRAID TO FIGHT.
BIG...
...MISTAKE...

...LIFE TO EAT...

NO.
I USED TO BE SCARED ALL THE TIME. I HID AWAY, TOO FRIGHTENED TO DO ANYTHING. BE AROUND ANYONE.
TOO AFRAID OF THE WHOLE WORLD.

...FEAR...
...SPREAD FEAR TO TASTE...
NYC TAXI

I CAN'T... I *CAN'T* RUN AWAY.
IT WILL FIND ME, ***GET*** ME IF I DO...!

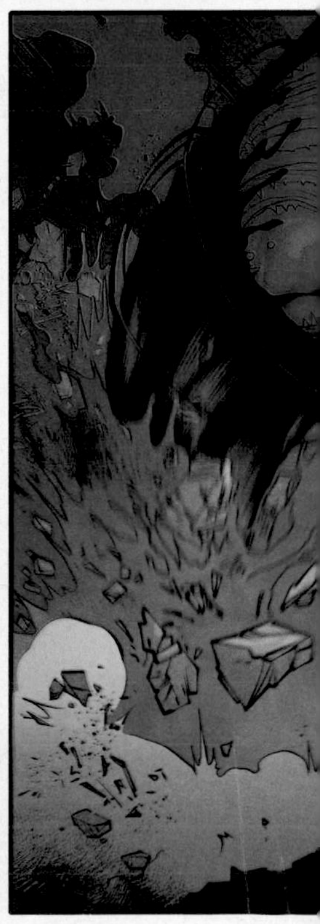

STATE OF FEAR PART ONE

BRYAN HITCH
WRITER

MATTHEW CLARK + TOM DERENICK
PENCILLERS

SEAN PARSO[illegible]S + TREVOR SCOTT
INKERS

ADRIANO LUCAS
COLORIST

RICHARD STARKINGS + COMICRAFT
LETTERING

TONY DANIEL + TOMEU MOREY
COVER

YANICK PAQUETTE + NATHAN FAIRBAIRN
VARIANT COVER

AMEDEO TURTURRO + DIEGO LOPEZ
ASSISTANT EDITORS

BRIAN CUNNINGHAM
EDITOR

BRIAN CUNNINGHAM Editor - Original Series • **AMEDEO TURTURRO DIEGO LOPEZ** Assistant Editors - Original Series
JEB WOODARD Group Editor - Collected Editions • **ROBIN WILDMAN** Editor - Collected Edition
STEVE COOK Design Director - Books • **DAMIAN RYLAND** Publication Design

BOB HARRAS Senior VP - Editor-in-Chief, DC Comics

DIANE NELSON President • **DAN DiDIO** Publisher • **JIM LEE** Publisher • **GEOFF JOHNS** President & Chief Creative Officer
AMIT DESAI Executive VP - Business & Marketing Strategy, Direct to Consumer & Global Franchise Management
SAM ADES Senior VP - Direct to Consumer • **BOBBIE CHASE** VP - Talent Development
MARK CHIARELLO Senior VP - Art, Design & Collected Editions • **JOHN CUNNINGHAM** Senior VP - Sales & Trade Marketing
ANNE DePIES Senior VP - Business Strategy, Finance & Administration • **DON FALLETTI** VP - Manufacturing Operations
LAWRENCE GANEM VP - Editorial Administration & Talent Relations • **ALISON GILL** Senior VP - Manufacturing & Operations
HANK KANALZ Senior VP - Editorial Strategy & Administration • **JAY KOGAN** VP - Legal Affairs
THOMAS LOFTUS VP - Business Affairs • **JACK MAHAN** VP - Business Affairs
NICK J. NAPOLITANO VP - Manufacturing Administration • **EDDIE SCANNELL** VP - Consumer Marketing
COURTNEY SIMMONS Senior VP - Publicity & Communications
JIM (SKI) SOKOLOWSKI VP - Comic Book Specialty Sales & Trade Marketing
NANCY SPEARS VP - Mass, Book, Digital Sales & Trade Marketing

JUSTICE LEAGUE VOLUME 2: OUTBREAK

DC Comics, 2900 West Alameda Ave., Burbank, CA 91505
Printed by LSC Communications, Salem, VA, USA. 3/24/17. First Printing.
ISBN: 978-1-4012-6870-1

Library of Congress Cataloging-in-Publication Data is available.

JUSTICE LEAGUE
VOL.2 OUTBREAK

BRYAN HITCH
writer

NEIL EDWARDS
JESUS MERINO * MATTHEW CLARK * TOM DERENICK
pencillers

DANIEL HENRIQUES
ANDY OWENS * SEAN PARSONS * TREVOR SCOTT
inkers

ADRIANO LUCAS
TONY AVIÑA
colorists

RICHARD STARKINGS & COMICRAFT
letterers

TONY S. DANIEL, SANDU FLOREA & TOMEU MOREY
collection cover artists

SUPERMAN created by **JERRY SIEGEL** and **JOE SHUSTER**
By special arrangement with the Jerry Siegel family